THE FLORIDA FOOD FOREST COOKBOOK

by Rachel The Good
with David The Good

Published by Good Books Publishing.

To my grandma, Sally, and to my mom, Kathy.
The two best cooks and hostesses I know.

Introduction by David

After the first edition of *Create Your Own Florida Food Forest* was published back in 2015, we started getting questions about how we eat "all the weird stuff" we grow. These questions intensified after the release of *Totally Crazy Easy Florida Gardening* later that same year. I tried to explain that Rachel did most of the cooking, and that I wasn't really great at recipes, and that...

"Have Rachel write a cookbook!" came the reply.

So I asked her if she would. She liked the idea, yet she was always busy making meals, homeschooling children and taking care of babies. Rachel was definitely good at figuring out what to do with strange tropical roots, fruits and shoots – but she just didn't have the time to write. Yet over the years, she's collected recipes here and there and written some of her own. And I've done the same, as we've tested different crops and learned to prepare them for the table.

Now, at long last, the two of us decided that if another year went by, it would be an entire decade of planning to eventually write this cookbook. That's just too long!

This simple little book contains the recipes Rachel has used to feed our large family. Much of our food comes from the backyard. In 2023, for example, we harvested 2,573lbs of vegetables, plus 14lbs of chicken, 449lbs of pork, 2,467 eggs and 434 gallons of milk. Some of our vegetables are common ones that everyone knows how to use, like broccoli, potatoes and carrots. But other vegetables we grow are less familiar to most Americans, like longevity spinach, true yams, Seminole pumpkins, ivy gourd, kangkong, daikons and cucuzza squash.

Our focus is growing high-yield vegetables that were adapted to the climate of Florida, instead of many vegetables common to the American diet.

We have adapted our palettes to fit the plants that love to grow here. Many of these - vegetables can be substituted for similar vegetables, which gave us a good place to start. True yams and cassava can often fill in for potatoes, and greens like katuk and longevity spinach can fill in for common spinach.

Some vegetables are in a class all their own and we adapted accordingly.

Thank you for encouraging Rachel to write this book – may it be useful in using the great bounty you reap from your Florida backyard garden or food forest.

Bon appetit!

Introduction by Rachel

Have you ever had your husband walk through the door with a bunch of international produce, the names of which you can't even pronounce, and say something like, "Woohoo! Look what's ready for harvest! We could eat for a couple of months on this, isn't it great?!"

Sounds a little overwhelming! This is where the spatula meets the pan.

It's all well and good to grow the majority of your own food, but you *actually have to eat it as well.*

When you go to the grocery store, you mostly see the same produce your mom saw when she was a kid. White potatoes, carrots, broccoli, tomatoes. We grew up learning how to cook them.

Before I married David, I had never heard of African yams, moringa or cassava. But suddenly we were growing them in our garden and I was tasked with figuring out what on earth to do with them!

And *Oh the abundance*!

David has a knack for discovering which crops will grow well in our climate. And it just so happens that most of them were unfamiliar to me. And he often plants tons of them. Sometimes literally.

I often think of the TV show Iron Chef.

It's 4:00PM. Now make a decent meal with pumpkin and chaya that will WOW the judges (hungry, sometimes picky, children)!

This book contains some of my attempts to feed the gang from the garden. The key is experimentation. Taste your vegetables. What do they remind you of? How can you use that to your advantage? Have fun with it!

After the garden, the next stop is the kitchen. So roll up your sleeves, get cooking and enjoy the journey.

List of Recipes

Amaranth & Friends

Florida's best-known amaranth variety is the obnoxious "pigweed," with its nasty spines and ability to show up everywhere if you let it go to seed. Its leaves are edible, but there are many better varieties and cousins that will grow in your garden and are better for the kitchen.

We've grown purple amaranth, Jamaican "callaloo" amaranth, *Golden Giant* amaranth, "Love Lies Bleeding" and the amaranth cousin *Celosia argentea*. We have also picked lamb's quarters from the yard and used its leaves in stir-fries, but we quit due to their very high oxalate content.

Amaranth is both a grain and a leaf crop. Some varieties are bred for their big edible leaves, and others for their seed.

Golden Giant yields a lot of seeds, which can be saved and used to make flour, or "popped" by heating on a hot skillet. At some point we need to experiment further with grain varieties. For now, we only grow amaranth for its edible leaves, along with saving seeds for future crops. Not that we need to, since they are always self-seeding around the nursery and garden!

Pinch out the middle of young amaranth plants to get them to branch, or just pick leaves as you have them.

Stir-fried Amaranth/Celosia

Heat some oil in a pan (we usually use lard, butter, ghee or coconut oil) and toss in fresh amaranth leaves. Saute the amaranth until it is deep green and well-wilted, then season with salt. You can also add garlic powder or onion powder or greens if so desired.

Amaranth and celosia greens are excellent in fried rice, or in scrambled eggs. They are also great in fajitas, Asian stir-fries, soups and more – use them as you would any cooked green.

Banana & Plantain

Bananas and plantains are some of the best staple crops on the planet. Bananas are a delicious fruit which can also be cooked green and used like a root crop. Likewise, plantains are good cooked green and starchy, or fried when ripe and sweet.

On our Caribbean homestead, we heavily relied on bananas and plantains. We were blessed to rent a small working farm during our first year there, and the owner had planted a big grove of bananas. That's where I'm harvesting bananas in the picture above! We could just walk down the stairs to the backyard, then open a little gate and enter our own private banana garden. There we had Cavendish, plantains and "rock figs," which were a fat little banana that was delicious when fully ripe – but not a minute before!

We ate so many bananas we should have turned into monkeys. It was amazing! Sometimes we'd have five or six big bunches ready at the same time. Our children would eat quite a few of these fresh, but we also used them green and in various recipes. Later, we planted our tropical Grocery Row Gardens with sixteen different varieties of bananas and plantains so we could keep the party growing!

If we lived in a location with less frost, we would plant dozens of bananas around the yard. From USDA Zone 9 north, it is harder to reap consistent harvests due to frosts taking the fruit before it ripens. South Florida and most coastal areas in the state are great places to grow bananas.

Keep them well-watered and fed and you'll have food year-round. Once you learn to use the green ones, you'll really love this versatile fruit!

Green Banana Porridge

Green banana porridge is a common Caribbean breakfast. It sounds so odd you just have to give it a try! Believe me, it's delicious!!! Almost like cream of wheat, but gluten-free!

Ingredients:

4 green bananas
1 c. coconut milk
1 c. whole milk
2 c. water
½ t. salt
1 t. vanilla extract
½ t. cinnamon
½ t. nutmeg
¼ t. allspice
½ c. sweetened condensed milk or to taste

Cut the ends off the bananas and score lengthwise once or twice. Peel the bananas. Put them in the blender with the coconut milk and whole milk and as much of the water as you can fit into the blender. Blend until very smooth.

Put this into a pot and add the rest of the water if you weren't able to get it into the blender previously. Turn it on medium-high/high and bring to a boil, string frequently so it doesn't stick and burn. If it seems to be cooking too hot and fast, turn the temp down. The porridge will start to thicken.

When thick, turn the heat off and add the spices and sweetened condensed milk. Taste and adjust seasonings to your liking.

Serve to smiling children.

Yield: 4 servings

Fried Plantains (Ripe)

Ingredients:

Fully ripe plantains (usually yellow, with lots of black!)
Lard (or tallow, bacon fat, coconut oil or ghee)

Cut the ends off the plantains and score lengthwise two or three times.

Peel the plantains.

Lay them on the cutting board so that they look like they are making a frowning face at you. Then hold your knife at about a 45 degree angle and cut the plantains on the bias.

Put a pan on high/medium-high and melt about an inch worth of fat in it.

When the fat is hot, place the sliced plantains into it.

You want enough space around the slices so that they will get nice and brown and it will be easy to get them in and out of the pan. They will cook very quickly.

Almost as soon as you get the last one in the pan, you will need to flip the first one.

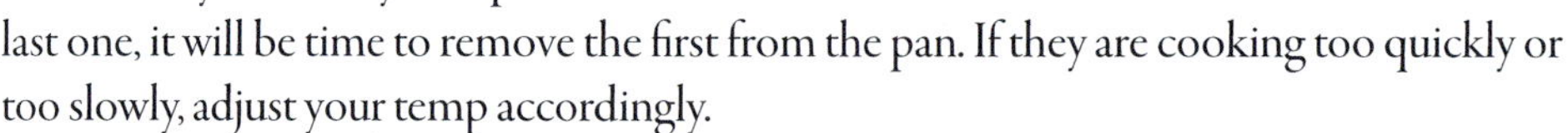

And by the time you flip the last one, it will be time to remove the first from the pan. If they are cooking too quickly or too slowly, adjust your temp accordingly.

These are a wonderful snack all on their own. But they also make a nice side dish with re-fried beans and rice.

Fried Plantains or Tostones (savory)

Ingredients:

Green plantains
Lard (or tallow, bacon fat, coconut oil or ghee)

Cut the plantains like you would do in preparation for frying them fully ripe and sweet. (Cut the ends off and score them about three times lengthwise and peel.) Then cut them on the bias as you do for sweet ones.

Heat about an inch of fat on high/medium-high and put the sliced plantains into the fat.

Fry them for a minute and then flip.

Cook another minute. They should be ever so slightly browned.

If not, adjust your temperature so that they achieve this color in about 1 minute per side.

Remove from the pan and put them on a plate.

Using a flat bottomed glass, press down on the plantain slices to flatten them. Place them back into the hot fat and cook for one minute.

Flip.

Cook for another minute.

Remove from the pan and sprinkle with salt.

These are really good dipped into just about anything imaginable: homemade mayo, guacamole, salsa, sour cream, hummus...

Alternately, instead of slicing the plantains on the bias, you can fry the entire peeled plantain for about a minute, flip it, cook for another minute, remove from the fat, flatten it with a glass, put back into the hot fat and fry again one minute each side!

Banana and Seminole Pumpkin Smoothies

Smoothies are a quick way to make a meal replacement, and to add extra nutrients to your diet in a fun way. If you're working out and want to add protein, it's also easy to add some peanut butter and/or protein powder to your smoothie.

Seminole pumpkins are quite delicious in smoothies. When mixed with banana and spices, it's like drinking a healthy slice of pie!

Ingredients:

~ ¾ c. Seminole pumpkin, rough mash
1 ripe frozen banana, broken into 3 parts
whole milk
2 eggs
~1/4 c. peanut butter (optional)
a pinch of kelp meal (optional)
a couple of dashes of cinnamon
a pinch of allspice (optional)
a pinch of nutmeg (optional)
splash of vanilla

For the pumpkin:

As noted under Seminole pumpkins, just cut the pumpkin in half, remove the seeds and bake in a 400 degree oven for about 45 minutes. It is finished when a butter knife goes in easily. When cool enough to handle, scoop out the pumpkin and rough mash it into a container. Do this the day before you want to enjoy your smoothie so the pumpkin has time to cool. (Alternately, you can use left-over pumpkin from supper the night before).

For the rest of the smoothie/the next day:

Place about ¾ c. of the roughly mashed pumpkin into a blender along with the frozen banana, eggs, kelp meal, cinnamon and vanilla. Blend this. Because smoothie density is dependent upon personal preferences, add milk until you reach your desired consistency. We often add kelp meal for extra nutrition. It just blends right in without being offensive to the palate.

**David's note: This feeds about 1 greedy 2 year old.*

Cabbage

Cabbage grows decently in Florida in the cool season. Sometimes we've grown quite a lot of it, and other years it gets destroyed by cabbage moths. When we get a lot of it, though, we love to make sauerkraut.

We've been making our own sauerkraut for a long time. It's not scary, and it's not "rotten cabbage" as detractors like to say. Any more than yogurt is "rotten milk" or wine is "spoiled grape juice," or apple cider vinegar is "putrid apple blood." It's a living, delicious, pro-biotic food with more nutritional value than raw cabbage.

Mason Jar Sauerkraut

First, get some cabbages, sea salt or kosher salt (not iodized salt!), and a nice jar. Chop the cabbages up and stuff in the jar.

Cover with brine.

To make brine, mix non-chlorinated water (if available) with salt. In the tropics we used a ratio of 4 tablespoons of salt per quart of water; however, if you are in a cooler climate that is excessive! Here we use 3 tablespoons. In Tennessee during winter we used 2 tablespoons. You can get away with just a tablespoon or two per quart if the weather is cold out.

Despite my best efforts, I have not had luck getting salt to "extract the juices from the cabbage" in enough quantity to work, despite that being related as the "proper" way to make sauerkraut in some recipes. Instead, we just dump in brine.

Note that we do not add vinegar. Just brine. Bacteria will proliferate in the mixture and make it sour for you – and they're the magic ingredient that makes sauerkraut an exceptionally healthy food.

Once you've filled your jar with cabbage and covered with brine (not to the top!), place a glass fermenter weight on top of the cabbage and screw on a fermentation lid. The fermentation lid has a one-way valve, allowing the gasses that form during fermentation to escape, but keep air out.

After 24 hours you have a live culture food, ready to provide your body with good probiotics. However, your sauerkraut will still taste pretty bland. Depending upon the temperature of your kitchen, it will take more or less days to sour to your liking. Taste a little every day until it reaches your desired flavor. Once you reach that sweet spot, put a regular Mason jar lid on it and keep it in the refrigerator.

I haven't always used these fermentation weights and lids. A family member gave me some and I tried them out. It was a complete game changer! I like to be frugal, so believe me when I tell you, these are worth it!

If this isn't enough to convince you and you're still scared of sauerkraut – it's okay. Just make coleslaw like a normal person.

Calamondin

The calamondin is a sour citrus fruit that looks like a little tangerine. David's grandmother had one in her yard when he was little. She told him it was the best fruit for marmalade. Even though calamondin skin is slightly sweet, the fruit wedges inside are incredibly sour.

Children like to eat them, as they are like Warheads sour candy, but most adults won't taste them again after a first try!

Calamondin is best used as a replacement for lime or lemon in recipe (it makes a refreshing lemonade) and the juice is exceptionally good in cocktails, such as:

Calamondin Whiskey Sours

Ingredients:

1 Part Calamondin Juice
1 Part Simple Syrup
2 Parts Bourbon

Pour into a shaker with ice and shake vigorously, then strain into tumblers of ice. Garnish with a maraschino cherry or a wedge of calamondin if desired.

Canna

Canna lilies are a very common landscape flower which also has edible roots and blooms. Don't mix them up with "calla lilies," which are poisonous.

Canna flowers can be tossed in salads or used as a garnish. They are delicate and slightly sweet. The roots on some species taste better than others. The variety known as "achira," (*Canna edulis*) has large roots that can be used like potatoes.

Some of the ornamental types have roots that are too small and filled with threads to be much use. They can still be cooked or eaten raw. Just chew the starch out of the threads.

This knowledge could be important if communists lock you up in a flower garden and you don't have anything to eat.

Cassava

Cassava grows in spokes out from a central stem. If you have good-sized roots (2" diameter or so, or larger), chop the whole plant down and carefully pull up your roots from the soil. Do your best to avoid damaging the roots as you dig around the plant. They are easy to chop through with a shovel.

After digging, cassava roots only keep for a few days before starting to darken and spoil inside, so dig them when you need them or leave them in the ground. You can sneak a root or two from the sides of a growing plant if you do not want to dig the whole thing, but generally we just dig a plant all at once, peel the roots, plant the canes we cut down, then process the roots for cooking. If we have a lot of roots, we'll often process them by removing the peels and the threads inside, then we'll bag and freeze them to use later.

Before you can do anything more interesting with cassava, you must first boil it. This is done to off-gas the cyanide found in the vegetable.

That said, don't be afraid of cassava! In our culture we grow up learning the common foods not to eat raw: white potatoes, dry beans, chicken. People in Africa and South America, likewise, teach their children that cassava needs to be well-cooked.

Here's how to boil it.

If you've just dug up your cassava roots, rinse off the dirt and cut the ends off. Then score the root, lengthwise, and peel off the brown, bark-like skin. Cut the cassava into sections about 4 inches long.

Put the cassava into a pot and fill it with water to cover and a generous amount of salt. Turn to high and boil for at least 20 minutes. Test the cassava by poking it with a butter knife. When it is cooked, you should feel about as much resistance as you wold from a baked potato. (Maybe slightly more. But if you've boiled it for at least 20 minutes it will be safe.)

Cassava leaves can also be boiled for twenty minutes and eaten. Younger leaves are more tender, but all of them are a bit papery, though high in protein and nutrients. Recently we put some through the blender then cooked them into a soup. It was edible. Africans often have recipes for the leaves but we don't use them often as we have other more palatable greens we prefer.

Cassava can be sliced into chunks and cooked in stew, or boiled and mashed like mashed potatoes. It's thicker and stickier than mashed potatoes, though! They have about twice the calories of a potato and will keep you full for a long time. Cassava is really chewy and dense.

Our favorite way to eat cassava is as cassava fries. Sometimes they become a meal all by themselves, and because cassava is so filling, no one goes away hungry.

Cassava Fries

Ingredients:

Cassava
Cooking oil (Lard/tallow/bacon fat/ghee/coconut oil)

First, boil your fresh cassava roots until fork-tender (as above). Then remove them from the pot. When cooled enough to handle, cut the pieces in half (or quarters if they are very large in diameter) and pan fry them in hot lard/tallow/bacon fat/ghee/coconut oil. Or place them on a sheet pan and brush with melted lard/tallow/bacon fat/ghee/coconut oil and broil at 400 degrees until beautifully brown and crispy. You've just made cassava fries!

Sprinkle with salt or serve with your favorite dipping sauce. Homemade mayo (see "Mayonnaise") mixed with some sweet relish, a dash of mustard and some ketchup to taste makes a really good dipping sauce that tastes rather like that weird pinky-orange sauce on Big Macs.

I don't like ketchup, so I skip that, but David and the kids like it. I prefer a mixture of mayo and mustard.

Chaya

Chaya, also known as "Mexican tree spinach," is a hearty leaf vegetable related to cassava.

It's a perennial shrub that can grow into a small tree in South Florida. In Central Florida, frosts will knock it back but it recovers. In North Florida, it needs a little protection from the harshest cold or it may die forever. If mulched, it usually recovers after winter and grows back from the ground. Down in the Caribbean we planted a hedge of it at the front of our property, then harvested baskets of leaves whenever we wanted a green vegetable to add to a meal.

There is a wilder form with somewhat tougher leaves, but which blooms regularly – and a more refined variety with tender leaves which we've never seen bloom.

Like cassava, chaya is easy to propagate from cuttings. Take some cuttings and let the cuts heal in the shade for a few days, then plant them in soil. 6-12" pieces work great.

Unlike many greens, chaya should not be eaten raw as it contains some cyanide in the leaves. When cooked, however, it is perfectly safe to eat.

To prepare, just boil chaya leaves in water for twenty minutes. Do not cook them in an aluminum pot, as they are reported to react with the aluminum.

Chaya leaves are a good stand-in for collard greens but taste even better. Sometimes we'll pick a mess of them, then boil and eat them as a meal in themselves.

Chestnut

Blight-resistant chestnuts like the *Dunstan* and the Chinese chestnut are easy to grow from Central Florida on north. The *Dunstan* chestnut was bred near Gainesville and we've seen a beautiful orchard of them at Chestnut Hill Tree Farm.

Chestnut trees are sometimes planted to attract deer to hunting camps in the Panhandle, but they are great for humans to eat as well.

Despite what Christmas songs might lead you to believe, we have not had success roasting them on an open fire. Instead, we remove the chestnuts from their spiny shells and score an "X" on the bottom with a knife. Boil until soft. The skin splits open easily at this point. The flavor is nutty, and somewhat like a white sweet potato. It is reported that they can also be dried and made into flour. We haven't had enough nuts to experiment further, but we look forward to doing so once our trees get bigger and start really producing.

Coconut

Coconuts are a staple crop from the tropics with many uses.

Sadly, it is only possible to grow them in frost-free locations. If you live in South Florida, plant a half-dozen for us!

Coconut Water

When I was a kid growing up in South Florida, we thought the clear liquid in the coconut was coconut milk. It wasn't until we moved to the Caribbean that I learned the difference between coconut water and coconut milk. The coconut water, that clear liquid, is a natural electrolyte drink. It has also been used as an intravenous hydration fluid (IV fluid) in cases where other forms of IV fluid were scarce.

To get the coconut water out of the coconut, get your strong, machete wielding husband to knock off the pointy end of the coconut, leaving a small opening into the coconut. Here you can insert a straw or bring it directly to your mouth or pour the water into a glass to enjoy.

If the coconut is young (on the yellow rather than green or brown side) the interior coconut meat will not yet have hardened into the white coconut most people in the U.S. are familiar with. At this point the meat is refereed to as "coconut jelly."

Have your husband demonstrate his muscles again by cutting the coconut in half with the machete. Now you can take one of those chopped off pieces of the coconut husk (or a spoon) and scoop out the jelly and eat it. It's delicious! At the big outdoor market in Grande Anse, Grenada, men would bring pickup truck beds full of coconuts. You could buy a coconut and they would cut them open for you. You would stand there and drink the water and then hand the coconut back to them. They would then halve it for you and hand you the husk scoop. Then you could continue to walk the market, eating the jelly and enjoying the sunshine and smells of the Spice Island. Way better than a soda machine or a cooler of Gatorade!

Coconut Milk

Coconut milk is a white liquid made from blending the coconut with water. Choose a coconut that is green or brown and have your husband cut it open as described in the coconut water recipe. I like to reserve this coconut water to make the coconut milk. But if you have already enjoyed that on its own, you can use regular water too.

Use a butter knife to carefully pry the white flesh away from the brown, cup-like shell. If some of the brown, papery part of the shell remains on the meat, it is fine. You want the pieces to be about 2 to 3 inches across. They usually come out of the shell in sections about this size. But if not, just break or cut them into that size.

Put all the pieces into the blender. Add enough coconut water, or regular water, or both to the blender to cover the coconut.

Blend on low, working your way to the next highest speed, counting to 10 after each increase, until you reach your blender's highest speed.

Pour the resulting pulpy liquid through a fine mesh sieve. Squeeze the pulp with your hands or the back of a wooden spoon to get all that good stuff! The white liquid is coconut milk!

The left-over coconut pulp is delicious as well. It is a fun addition to oatmeal. I have not tried, but may in the future, putting it in granola or making coconut macaroons with it.

Coconut Oil

Coconut oil is widely used in Grenada. It was inexpensive to buy while we were there so I never tried making it myself. But I am familiar with the process:

Refrigerate coconut milk at least overnight (see recipe on how to make coconut milk). Now the coconut milk will have separated so that the coconut cream is at the top, looking like a sheet of ice on the top of a frozen lake.

Remove the solidified coconut cream to a pot and bring to a boil on the stove. Reduce to a simmer. Keep this simmering and watch it, string occasionally.

Curds will start to form and gradually sink to the bottom as they give up their oil. When the solids are slightly brown, pass the oil through a fine mesh sieve to separate.

Store the oil in a jar. You can keep it at room temperature or refrigerate it if you prefer.

Cocoplum

Cocoplums are a common beach-side plant that comes in both white and black-fruited varieties. On the island of Grenada it's known as "fat pork."

They're often used in "Florida-friendly" landscaping projects in portions of the state without frost. We've harvested them from along the beach, from parking lots, and multiple times from the long alleyway behind Family Thrift (now long-closed) in Lauderhill, Florida. Some landscaper planted a big hedge of them between the back of the thrift store and the apartment complex... and no one was easting them, so we did.

Some taste better than others. Pick them when ripe and eat them fresh off the shrub, chewing the flesh off the central pit. If you find some that taste great, plant the seeds in pots and they'll come up in a couple of months and you can grow your own!

As Green Deane writes on eattheweeds.com, "(Cocoplum) is made into jams and jellies. In Cuba it's manipulated into a sweet preserve that's served in Havana restaurants as a sobremesa or dessert. The large kernel removed from its shell is edible raw or cooked. Some think it has the faint flavor of almond. To me it tastes like granola. Many think the kernel is far better when the fruit and kernel are both pierced so the juice of the pulp is allowed to seep into the kernel."

Collards

Collards are an easy-to-grow relative of cabbage. They handle the heat pretty well and have a longer harvest season than some of their touchier cousins.

In the Deep South, you'll see pickup beds filled with collard greens for sale along the roadside in late spring.

Though they are too tough for fresh eating, boiled collard greens are a must-have at Southern family gatherings.

Collard Greens

This recipe utilizes the electric pressure cooker. What would normally take hours on the stove now takes only minutes!

Ingredients:

1 onion, chopped
4 cloves garlic, minced
salt and pepper to taste
1 package of bacon (size of your choice), cut into 1 inch pieces
3 large bunches of collard greens, stems removed and cut into bite sized pieces
1 c. homemade bone broth
1 t. red pepper flakes (optional)

Cook the bacon in the pressure cooker using the saute function. When cooked, remove the bacon from the pressure cooker and set aside. Leave all the fat in the pressure cooker. Now add the onion and garlic and saute. When the onion is translucent, add in the collards. You will have to add them in batches and wait for each batch to wilt before adding the next batch.

Add the bone broth and the optional red pepper flakes and stir. Put the lid on the pressure cooker and lock in place, setting the valve to "pressure". Cook on high pressure for 2 minutes.

Yield: 8-10 servings

**Each make and model of electric pressure cooker is different. You may find that your pressure cooker takes slightly longer. Adjust to your liking.*

Cucuzza

Cucuzza, aka Snake Gourd, is a lovely vegetable.

It is similar to "the Z word" but those that don't like the dreaded z@#$%^&*, like David, often like cucuzza.

Bonus points: it produces a larger vegetable than z@#$%^&* so you get more bang for your buck.

Cucuzza is the same species as birdhouse gourds, bushel gourds, dipper gourds, etc. (*Lagenaria siceraria*) except it has been selected to be eaten as a green vegetable. It sails through the heat and the rains and the pests and is almost a weed, unlike other summer squash. We enjoy it all summer long.

Sauteed Cucuzza

I like the simplicity and flavor of this sauteed cucuzza.

Ingredients:

1 cucuzza, at least about 3 feet long
butter
salt
Italian seasoning
garlic powder
onion powder

Cut the cuzuzza into manageable pieces, about 10 inches long or shorter if you reach a bend in the vegetable. Cut off the ends as well. Now peel the skin with a vegetable peeler. Cut each piece lengthwise and then cut those 2 pieces lengthwise. Chop into bite-sized pieces.

Heat a pan to medium and melt 2 T. butter. Add the cucuzza and saute. Sprinkle with salt, pepper, Italian seasoning, garlic powder and onion powder. Saute the cucuzza until soft.

Taste and adjust seasonings. I tend to go heavy on the salt, pepper, Italian seasoning, onion powder and garlic powder.

Note: If, when peeling the cucuzza you find it hard to peel, the vegetable is probably too mature to make a good meal. Its flesh and seeds will most likely be too hard and woody to enjoy. Feed it to your animals.

Cucuzza Casserole

Because the cucuzza is so similar to z@#$%^&*, I find that you can replace it in your favorite "summer squash" recipe. Feel free to replace it in yours, or take this recipe.

Ingredients:

6 T. butter
about 3 lbs. Cucuzza, ends cut off, peeled and chopped into bite sized pieces
1 medium onion, chopped
2 t. salt
2 eggs, lightly beaten
8 oz sour cream, room temperature
4 oz sharp cheddar cheese, shredded
2 oz Swiss cheese, shredded (about ½ cup)
½ c. mayonnaise
2 t. thyme
½ t. pepper
2 sleeves Ritz crackers, coarsely crushed (alternately you could use cubed or broken homemade bread, or even homemade or store bought breadcrumbs)
1 oz Parmesan cheese (about ¼ c)

Saute the cucuzza in 2-3 T. of the butter and a pinch of salt until just barely tender. Transfer it to a colander and allow it to drain off as much liquid as possible while you work on the next step.

Preheat the oven to 350 degrees F and grease an 11 x 7" casserole dish. You can use a different sized casserole. It's not the end of the world, just know that it may take more or less time and your casserole to topping ratio will be different.

In a large bowl, place the onion, 2 t. salt, eggs, sour cream, cheddar cheese, Swiss cheese, mayo, thyme and pepper. Stir to combine. Add the cucuzza and stir gently. Pour this into your casserole dish.

Melt the remaining butter (3-4 T.). In a bowl, place your crushed Ritz crackers, melted butter and Parmesan cheese. Sprinkle this on top of the cucuzza casserole. Bake for 20 minutes. It is finished when it's bubbly and irresistible!

Yields 8 servings

**Note: In an effort to make Seminole pumpkin more accessible to my family, I have also substituted pureed pumpkin for the cucuzza. It is a good use for any left-over pumpkin you might have from the day before.*

Daikon Radish

Daikon radishes are generally milder than their small, red, globular relatives. Their large size is perfect for feeding a quantity of people with only a handful of plants.

They are easy to grow in Florida during the cool season and can be harvested over a much longer period than salad radishes. Over the years, they have become a vegetable we really enjoy and look forward to harvesting in season.

Roasted Daikons

1 lb daikon radishes
1 package of bacon (any size you like)
1 ½ t. balsamic vinegar (feel free to substitute some other exotic type of vinegar here)
1 ½ T. cane syrup or maple syrup
salt and pepper to taste

Lay all the bacon onto a tray and cook in a 400 degree oven until done. The time depends upon the thickness of the bacon.

I usually cook it for 8-10 minutes and then check. When done, remove the bacon to a paper towel lined plate and pour off (but reserve!) the grease.

Remove the tops and bottoms of the daikons and peel. Then cut them into bite sized chunks.

Put them in the pan and drizzle with 3-4 T. of the bacon grease. Just eyeball it. Use more if you feel like it. Raise the temperature of the oven to 425 degrees.

Roast the daikons until they are just barely starting to brown.

Add the balsamic vinegar, cane syrup (or maple syrup) and salt and pepper to taste. Toss them around a bit in the pan.

Put the pan back into the oven and continue to roast until they are a deep and delicious brown and your kitchen smells like you want to lick the air.

Crumble the bacon onto the top and serve.

Yield: 4 servings

**Note: Save any unused bacon grease in a jar in the refrigerator. Use it to cook pretty much anything.*

Live-Fermented Daikons

Daikons are a key ingredient in traditional Korean kimchi. Other ingredients include Napa cabbage, brined shrimp, anchovy sauce, hot pepper, ginger, garlic and more. We have not made good kimchi yet, as we rarely seem to have all the ingredients needed. Yet we have made a variety of simple and delicious ferments with daikon radishes.

The simplest is simply to chop up a few big radishes and put them in a canning jar, then cover them with salt brine and a fermentation weight and lid. We use 2-3 tablespoons of salt per quart of water to make the brine, just as we do with sauerkraut.

Pour that brine over your chopped daikons and use the glass fermentation weight to press them down beneath the brine. Then screw on the fermentation lid.

In about three days of sitting on the counter, the daikons will start to taste sour. In a few more days, they're usually perfect. They take a little longer than the sauerkraut because they are cut into chunks whereas the cabbage is cut into a finer slice. At that point, we switch out the fermentation lid for a regular Mason jar lid and put them in the fridge. That way fermentation slows down and they keep their sharp, tangy, pickled flavor without getting weird and musty. You can taste them daily after three days, since ambient temperatures and the bacteria in your kitchen will vary the speed of fermentation.

Just put them in the fridge once they taste nicely pickled. They'll keep a long, long time under refrigeration.

Sometimes we mix daikons and cabbage together to make a type of sauerkraut. We've also added garlic, mustard seeds, black pepper, rosemary and other garden herbs, hot red pepper flakes and more.

Once you know how to make a basic ferment, just play around and see what you like.

Eggplant

Eggplant is generally easy to grow in Florida. It likes the heat and can be quite productive. Sometimes too productive! Not everyone likes it, but if you do, it's an excellent addition to your Florida garden. We really enjoy ours through the summer.

We start seedlings in February/March, then plant them out in the garden in April. From there, they run all the way through the summer, making us plenty of eggplants to eat – and plenty more to give away.

There are many varieties of eggplant, from big Italian types to long Asian types. There are white, purple and even green cultivars.

All of them are delicious when covered in parmesan!

Chicken and Eggplant Parmesan Casserole

I love casseroles and I'm not ashamed to admit it! This one was born out of my desire to feed my family the eggplant from our garden in a way even the pickiest would enjoy, and a desire *not* to bread and fry food on the stove. I don't quite have this recipe down in exact measurements yet. I know all the ingredients and kind of just feel it. You'll get it!

Ingredients:

1 chicken
about 2 lbs of eggplant
butter/lard/coconut oil/bacon fat/tallow/ghee (from here on I will refer to this as "fat." Use whichever you have and feel is best
1 can Italian seasoned breadcrumbs
crushed tomatoes, several cans
powdered Parmesan cheese
mozzarella cheese, grated
salt and pepper to taste
Italian seasoning
garlic powder
onion powder

Cook the chicken in the electric pressure cooker, with 1 c. water for about an hour. A tougher bird will require this long. A more tender one might take less time. When it is finished, remove it from the pressure cooker and let it cool for about 10 minutes. Then debone the chicken and roughly chop the meat.

Preheat the oven to 350 degrees.

Peel the eggplant and chop it into bite-sized pieces. Saute the eggplant in some fat. It will soak it up nicely so you will need to add more as the eggplant cooks. Saute until it is tender.

In a casserole pan, put all the chopped chicken. Sprinkle with salt, pepper, Italian seasoning, garlic powder and onion powder to your liking. I'm usually pretty heavy handed with this. Sprinkle generously with breadcrumbs. Then pour enough crushed tomatoes on top to cover the chicken. Sprinkle with the grated mozzarella and dust with the Parmesan. Next, layer on the eggplant. Sprinkle this with the salt, pepper, Italian seasoning, garlic powder and onion powder. And top with the breadcrumbs, crushed tomatoes, mozzarella and Parmesan. Bake for 20 minutes or until bubbly and beautiful. Let rest for about 10 minutes before serving.

Yield: about 4 servings

Everglades Tomatoes

Everglades tomatoes are the easiest tomato you can grow in Florida. They are half-wild, with small fruit that explode with big tomato flavor.

The plants sprawl across the ground and resist trellising – and they self-seed prolifically.

Because the fruits are so small, they aren't the best for making sauces; however, if you have the patience, you can gather multiple cups of them and give it a go. We've done it, and the flavor is exceptionally good.

One of our favorite ways to use Everglades tomatoes is to toss them whole into stir-fries, letting them heat up and pop. They are also very good added to scrambled eggs and salsas.

Green Tomatoes

Florida is a tough place to grow big backyard tomatoes. Many times they'll be struck with rot or disease or insect issues as they ripen. However, green tomatoes are a good vegetable in their own right. There are quite a few seasons where we didn't do great with getting large, ripe tomatoes – but we could get plenty of green tomatoes by picking them before the bugs attacked.

You can chop green tomatoes into pieces and saute them with eggs and fried rice, or add them to casseroles and other dishes. They are also a common ingredient in our hot pepper sauce (see "hot peppers" for that recipe).

Any recipe calling for "tomatillos" can use green tomatoes instead.

Hot Peppers

Hot peppers are easy to grow in Florida, and in areas with mild and mostly frost-free winters, they can be grown as a short-lived perennial shrub.

Using a lot of hot peppers in recipes can be tough unless you have a high pain tolerance; however, they are excellent for seasoning, sauces and dried ground pepper.

Smoked Hot Pepper Sauce

About every other year, we grow a lot of hot peppers for sauce making.

The best we've made is the smoked hot pepper sauce David invented a decade ago when we had way too many peppers and green tomatoes in the garden and a frost was on the way. He threw all the peppers in, green and red!

Cayenne peppers are a great base for this sauce, but we've also added varying amounts of pepperoncini, tabasco, jalapenos, habaneros, poblanos, paprikas and other peppers. If we have them, we also often throw in a handful of green tomatoes.

Just pick at least a quart or so of peppers and a few tomatoes if you like, then smoke them.

It's nice to have a smoker, but in a pinch David made a redneck smoker that worked fine. This was just a big pot with a wire basket hanging at the top. In the bottom of the pot, we put some wood chips, then filled the basket with our peppers and green tomatoes. He covered this all with a lid, then put it on a burner outside. The wood chips started smoking within a few minutes, and we added more as they burned out, smoking the peppers for an hour or two.

Once they're nice and smoked, let the peppers cool, then chop off the stems.

Throw your peppers and tomatoes in the blender, then cover with vinegar. If you like cider vinegar, use that. We've also used white wine vinegar and it was excellent. But even white distilled vinegar is just fine.

Run the blender, then add a tablespoon of salt. Add more to taste, if necessary. We also add a tablespoon of sugar or two – also to taste. We don't want the sauce sweet, but a hint of sweetness against the vinegar and salt heightens the flavor.

Finally, add a tablespoon of garlic powder. Or throw some garlic cloves in the blender.

Blend the sauce a final time to mix it all in, then pour your freshly minted smoky homemade hot pepper sauce into half-pint jars for canning.

Because this sauce is vinegar-based, we water bath can these for twenty minutes and figure they're safe enough for rock and roll.

This sauce has a rich, smoky-hot flavor that will make you want to eat more and more of it. It's exceptional on eggs and marvelous when served with tortilla chips. Just opening a jar scents the room with spicy smoky goodness.

Pickled Jalapeno Slices

One year David started a bunch of jalapeno peppers in the greenhouse, hoping to sell the little plants at the farmer's market. They weren't as popular as he thought they'd be, so we ended up planting at least thirty in our fall garden. We ended up with so many peppers we could have started our own pepper spray company!

But instead of doing that, we made pepper sauce, and we also decided to make our own pickled jalapeno slices. The flavor... oh my goodness... the flavor! These pickled jalapeno pepper slices are incredibly good.

Are you ready to can your own? Here's how we did it.

Ingredients:

4 lbs jalapenos
1/2 cup sugar
1/4 cup sea salt
1 ½ quarts vinegar
1 ½ quarts water
6 cloves garlic
Dash of turmeric
2-3 hot red peppers (any kind)
Sprinkle of pepper
Sprinkle of mustard seeds

First, wash your canning jars and lids so they're ready to go. Then, pick about 4 lbs of jalapeno peppers We like to pick mostly green ones for this recipe, but we leave a few reds to ripen here and there. They add color and a sweetness to the mix. We also toss in a couple of cayennes when we have them.

Chop your jalapenos into slices. We usually chop them in perfect circles; however, ellipsoids also fall inside pickled jalapeno orthodoxy.

Now start your brine. Mix the vinegar and water together, along with the salt and sugar, then bring to a boil. We throw in a dash more or less of salt and sugar according to taste. If it's zippy and a little salty and sweet, it's good. Our favorite salts are Himalayan pink salt, Celtic sea salt and Redmond salt. Any of those will be better than factory-produced table salt.

Pack jalapenos into your jars as tightly as possible, then mash them down further and pack a few more in. Otherwise, when the jar is canned they'll get a little thin as they cook. Once the peppers are packed in, add a pinch of mustard seeds, a pinch of turmeric and a pinch of pepper, along with a chopped garlic clove in each jar.

Now it's time to pour on the brine. Having a jar funnel to load your mason jars is a big help at this point. Load the jars up with brine to about 1/4" from the top of the jar. Make sure you jog them around a bit since bubbles tend to hide inside the slices. Add more brine as necessary.

Screw the lids down tight.

Canning is easy when you're dealing with pickles. You're not going to get a horrible disease if you mess it up, since the vinegar keeps the food good and safe. We process our pepper pint jars for 10 minutes in our stock pot to seal them. Remember, you've already poured boiling brine over them, so they should be good and hot when they hit the boiling water bath. If you're scared of canning, just pop your jars into the refrigerator. They'll keep for longer than you think, thanks to the vinegar.

Yield: 6 Pints

Homemade Ground Cayenne Pepper

Have you ever tried a home-grown version of something and realized it utterly destroys your whole concept of how that food tastes? If you've had a sun-warmed red-ripe garden tomato or some golden-yolked free range farm eggs, you know what I mean. There's a richness to foods that aren't factory produced, shipped for miles or grown with chemicals in poor soil.

Homegrown-and-ground cayenne pepper is one of those foods. The flavor is simply incomparable. Yes, making your own takes a little work, but the results are worth every minute.

They're easy to grow and quite prolific. If you live in a frost-free area, you can grow them year-round and the bushes will produce for years. If, like I do, you live in an area that freezes, it's worth digging up plants from the garden and transplanting them to pots for the winter. They'll just keep on going, even in a sunny room or a greenhouse.

Harvesting peppers is easy – the stems break nicely and you can gather quite a few in a couple of minutes. Just be careful not to snap any branches on your plants or knock off peppers that are still developing. If you do, you can use those green ones in your sauces and dry pepper – they just don't have the same, sweet flavor the fully red peppers do.

Harvesting your own peppers allows you to wait for that perfect moment when they hit the high note of atomic redness. Watch for it!

We've all seen images of chili peppers hanging in strings, and though I like that idea, mine tend to get mold issues when I dry them traditionally. We don't have the arid climate that parts of Mexico has, so you risk spoiling your harvest if you don't get it dried quickly. For years I used an inexpensive Nesco column-style dehydrator that did a wonderful job. We have a bigger Excalibur now, but it really doesn't work much better.

When we dehydrate cayenne peppers, we don't even bother cutting them up. We just drop them in whole and let them dry overnight on the "vegetable" setting of 135 degrees F.

Once you've dried your peppers, there's only one more step.

If you want traditional red pepper flakes, you could just crumple your newly dehydrated peppers up with your fingers. They're really crunchy fresh from the dehydrator and it would be easy enough; however, I really like to go all the way and grind them fine.

To do that, you need another tool: a cheap coffee grinder.

We have a little Braun grinder. These aren't normally cheap. Ours came from a local thrift store where it was priced at a steep $3.50. Fortunately, pink tags were half-off that day so we got it for a more reasonable $1.75 (plus tax).

Clean your grinder out well with a damp cloth, then crunch a bunch of peppers into the top.

Pop on the top, push the button and the fun begins. It doesn't take long at all to grind up cayenne peppers into an amazing orange-red dust. I tilt the grinder a few times, tap it, zip it on and off a few times and run it again, just to make sure I don't have any pepper left un-ground.

WARNING:

When you open your grinder, hold your breath! And don't exhale, either. One time David exhaled slightly into the freshly-ground dust and it shot up into his face. He was instantly blind, and his eyes were on fire, and he could not open his eyelids! I had to lead him through the house to the shower so he could rinse the pepper from his eyes. Be careful!

Once you've ground up your pepper, you can store it in a jar. It's it beautiful?!

You can follow this same process with all kinds of pepper, including non-spicy paprika peppers or even nuclear-powered habaneros (we've done it with habaneros – it's flavorful and... dangerous).

Ground red pepper is excellent in chili and dusted on deviled eggs. It's also good for making cayenne tea when you wish to stop a persistent headache. If you have circulation or heart problems, it's also supposed to be good for keeping your vessels open and your hearty healthy.

But most of all, it's just delicious and we love it.

Ivy Gourd/Perennial Cucumber

Ivy gourd *(Coccinea grandis)* is a small easy-to-grow cucumber that produces continuously for years. It's also known as the "ivy gourd" or sometimes "tindoora" if you are talking with Indians (from India). They can be found occasionally in the wild and come in both male and female.

Only the latter fruits and it does not require a mate to make cucumbers. The resultant seeds will be sterile as well, which is good. Florida has enough invasive plants creeping around already!

Ivy gourds have little or no pest issues and produce in dry or wet conditions, producing large white blooms that give way to small mottled green cucumbers. If the cucumbers sit on the vine too long, they turn into an inedible sour, red mush. This vegetable is usually cooked but we also like them raw or pickled.

An isolated female ivy gourd in your garden, if kept from wandering off, can be controlled and generally won't be invasive.

If you have a male and a female, the seeds will be viable and are likely to get spread all over the place. We would not grow male plants as we do not want this species to invade all of Florida.

Female plants are propagated easily via cuttings, which root readily in moist soil in a shady spot. Down in South Florida, David knows of one particular planting of ivy gourds that has survived multiple landlords and absolutely no care and is still producing little cucumbers after almost 40 years of neglect. They were planted by a gardener along a fence... and are still there, growing back after weed-eating and mowing and... well, they're amazing!

Easy Ivy Gourd Pickles

Ingredients:

Green ivy gourds
Non-iodized salt (though iodized will still work)
Turmeric
Water
Other spices if desired

Pick fresh ivy gourds and slice them into quarters. If they are red inside, discard. You only want green ones.

Cut both ends off and add slices to a clean mason jar, along with fresh grated turmeric or turmeric powder (for color and health).

You can also add dill, black pepper, mustard seed or other herbs and spices you think would make the mix delicious.

Now make a brine with one pint of water and 1 ½ tablespoons of salt.

Pour the brine over the cucumber slices, covering them, then add a fermentation weight and cap with a fermentation lid. Leave the jar on counter for a few days, occasionally tasting a slice of cucumber. When they taste nice and sour, they're done!

You can put your pickles in the fridge to slow fermentation once they reach a good flavor. They'll keep for a long time.

If your cucumbers turn to mush, something has gone wrong with your fermentation. We've not had that happen unless we fail to add enough salt. Salt is like magic. It allows the good organisms to thrive and keeps the dangerous ones from making you sick.

Jamaican Sorrel/Florida Cranberry

Jamaican sorrel (*Hibiscus sabdariffa*), also known as Florida cranberry, is a large annual shrub in the hibiscus family that makes thick calyxes after blooming. These are used in a variety of drinks, sauces and teas. The calyxes are very popular in the Caribbean – we've had a rum punch made with it that is absolutely delicious. The leaves are also edible and tart and particularly good in Caesar salad.

When Thanksgiving comes around each year, I like to include as many things from our own homestead as possible. When we first grew Florida cranberries it seemed like a natural fit to substitute them for the real deal in my Mom's cranberry relish recipe.

The first time I served it to the extended family, they all had to be told it contained Florida cranberries. That's how closely the flavor of these strange fruits resembles their namesake! The following recipe is large enough to feed a crowd but it is easily halved.

Florida Cranberry Relish (AKA Jamaican Sorrel Relish)

Ingredients:

1 ½ c. orange or apple juice
1 1/3 c. sugar
1/2 t. ground cinnamon
1/2 t. ground nutmeg
a couple of dashes of ground cloves
24 oz. Florida cranberries
1 c. raisins (golden or ordinary)
1 c. chopped pecans

In a saucepan, combine juice, sugar, cinnamon, nutmeg and cloves. Cook over medium heat, stirring frequently until sugar is dissolved. Add Florida cranberries and raisins, bring to a boil.

Reduce heat, simmer 3-4 minutes.

Remove from heat, stir in chopped pecans. Chill for several hours.

I like to make Florida cranberry relish the day before as the flavors just get better the next day. One year I made extra, mixed it with cream cheese and we ate it on crackers as an appetizer.

Enjoy!

Kangkong

Kangkong is a relative of sweet potatoes. It is grown extensively in Southeast Asia. Instead of being grown for roots, it is grown for its leaves and tender shoots.

In some states it's classified as an invasive so getting plants from a nursery may be impossible. If you can't find it, make friends with internationals and show them pictures until someone gives you cuttings.

Kangkong leaves and young shoots are edible raw or cooked. Steamed, they taste mild with rich mushroom and asparagus undertones.

You sometimes see these greens at Asian markets, and if you're lucky, you'll find whole shoots you can plant to grow your own. They'll eat your entire pond, so watch out. Kangkong is very productive and VERY fast-growing. It's been reported to grow six inches a day under ideal conditions.

If those conditions are a kiddie pool in your backyard, that means you'll have lots and lots of fresh greens for the table! Just put some muck in a container without drainage and plant some kangkong. You'll be happy you have it. We particularly enjoy eating it in Spring when it starts to really run with the warm weather.

* *Kangkong image via whologwhy on Flickr. (cc license)*

Key Lime

Key limes just scream "Florida!" They really hate frost and must be protected if grown outside of South Florida. In North Florida, David grew them for me by espaliering a tree against the south-facing wall of our house. That's how we got these beauties:

Yet Key Lime pie is hotly contested in our house. I am partial to my Mom's recipe. David prefers the one his Grandma always made. But, since my family is actually *from* Florida, and I'm the one that does most of the cooking in our house, mine is the ONLY real and true Key Lime Pie recipe and it's all I fix. My Mom's pie is topped with meringue instead of whipped cream. Based upon my research, when the Florida Keys were being settled, and this pie was created, fresh milk was unobtainable in the Keys. Hence the lack of whipped cream. I will give you both recipes and you can make up your own mind.

Kathy's Key Lime Pie (Rachel's Mom)

Ingredients:

For the pie:

1, 9 inch graham cracker crust
½ c. key lime juice (4-6 key limes)
2 egg yolks (reserve whites for meringue)
1 can sweetened condensed milk

For the meringue:

2 egg whites (the ones separated and reserved from the above yolks)
¼ c. sugar
1 t. cream of tarter

Pie

Pre-heat oven to 300 degrees. Mix sweetened condensed milk and egg yolks with spoon. While stirring, slowly add the Key lime juice. Pour into pie shell.

Meringue

Beat egg whites with electric mixer until foamy. While beating add cream of tarter. Continue beating and slowly add sugar. Continue beating until you have stiff peaks. Pile on top of pie and smooth it to the edges of the crust. If the meringue touches the crust, it is less likely to pull away from the edge of the pie. If you wish you can press down all over the top of the meringue with a spoon and lift up quickly, creating little peaks across the top of the pie. Bake the pie for about 20 minutes. The top will be slightly browned. Chill completely before serving.

Grandma Marian's Key Lime Pie (David's Grandmother)

1, 9 inch graham cracker pie crust
1 can sweetened condensed milk
1/3 c. Key lime juice
3 eggs, separated
1 c. whipped cream, sweetened to taste

Mix sweetened condensed milk with beaten egg yolks. Add Key lime juice, slowly stirring. Beat the egg whites until stiff peaks form. Fold the egg whites into the Key lime mixture. Carefully place into the pie crust. Bake at 250 degrees for 15 minutes. Chill completely.

Serve with whipped cream.

Longevity & Okinawa Spinach

Longevity spinach (*Gynura procumbens*) was made for Florida. It's so healthy and easy to grow that you'll wonder how you went without it.

The leaves have an interesting fresh flavor, and it's a good salad stuffer or a cooked green.

Longevity spinach is a half-vining herbaceous perennial (try to say that three times fast!) that tolerates poor soil, drought and heat but benefits from water and compost.

You can easily start a lot of them by taking stem cuttings. Just break off a piece of stem, stick it in the ground, water it and it will root.

Longevity spiñach takes sun and shade well, but does not like the cold.

Its pretty purple-and-green cousin Okinawa spinach has a milder flavor but didn't grow as well in our North Florida gardens. Okinawa spinach seems to dislike cold and drought more than Longevity spinach, but we grow it any time we can because its quite pleasant to eat.

If Fall frosts are coming, take a few cuttings from your plants and put them in a pot to root, then plant them out again in Spring.

Down in South Florida, both plants are excellent year-round greens, both cooked and in salads.

And of course, in scrambled eggs.

With cheese.

And bacon!

Mango

David's grandparents had a mango tree in their backyard. He has fond memories of biking over to his Grandma and Grandpa's house with his brother Brian and eating frozen mango slices while watching *Star Trek* episodes on their Beta VCR.

My parents' house had a small mango orchard in the front yard that was probably planted some time in the 70s. They dropped mangoes all over – and my job was to mow the grass. I remember the sick-sweet smell of the rotten mangoes I hit with the mower. I hated mangoes and couldn't get that thought out of my head whenever I was offered a mango. It wasn't until we moved to Grenada that I found some mangoes I really loved.

Mangoes are best eaten fresh on a warm day, but a tree can produce so many fruit that it makes sense to save some of the harvest if you can! Preserving mangoes is like preserving the sunshine. Pull them out on a cool winter day and be instantly transported back to a warm, South Florida Summer; even if only in your mind.

Dehydrated Mangoes

Mangoes are easy to dehydrate. Peel them and cut them into slices, then lay them out on a drying rack and put them in a dehydrator on the "fruit" setting. They're like candy when dried! You don't need an expensive dehydrator to have good luck, either. We used an inexpensive circular column-type dehydrator for years before we ended up buying a bigger one later.

Once your mango slices are nice and dry, you can keep them in jars with the lids screwed tight, then put them away in the pantry. They keep a long time.

That is, unless you eat them all in a day. The danger of dehydrating mangoes is that they taste so good, sweet and chewy that you may end up devouring them all instead of storing them away. It's easy to eat ten mangoes worth of dried mango slices, so be careful.

Frozen Mangoes

Mangoes can be peeled, cut into pieces and frozen in bags for the future. This is what David's grandmother did. Any time she and Grandpa wanted a nice dessert, they would get a bag of mango slices from the freezer and put it out to thaw a little, then eat them half-frozen. David says they were better than ice cream on a hot day. This anole sure seemed to think so!

Faux Apple Pie (With Green Mangoes)

A friend of the family, Glenda, told me about this. When she sailed from South Africa to Florida, she got tired of all the tropical fruit and longed for apples, wishing she could make an apple pie. A friend suggested she get some green (unripe) mangoes and use them in place of the apples in her pie recipe. She said it worked beautifully!

When we were in the Caribbean and mangoes dropped from every tree, and apples were an expensive import, I got the opportunity to try it out for myself. Sure enough, it worked for me too.

If you have an apple pie recipe that is near and dear to your heart, by all means use that, and substitute the apples for green mangoes. If not, feel free to use my recipe.

Ingredients:

1 double crust pie pastry (feel free to use my recipe with the Pecan Pie)
Enough green (unripe) mangoes to equal 10 c. when sliced
½ c. white or brown sugar
¼ c. all purpose flour
1 T. lemon juice
1 ½ t. ground cinnamon
¼ t. ground allspice
¼ t. ground nutmeg
egg wash (optional): 1 egg beaten with 1 T. water
extra sugar for dusting (optional)

Line a 9" deep-dish pie pan with pie crust.

Peel mangoes* and slice into ¼ inch slices. Place mangoes into a large bowl and add sugar, flour, lemon juice, cinnamon, allspice and nutmeg. Stir.

Pour the mangoes into the pie shell. Place the top pie shell on top of the mangoes. If you wish, you can brush with the egg wash and dust with sugar.

Bake at 400 degrees for 25 minutes. Make a ring of aluminum foil and put over the pie crust edge to prevent burning. Reduce the temperature to 375 degrees and bake an additional 35-40 minutes. If the top of the pie looks to be getting too brown during this time, tent the entire pie with aluminum foil. When it's done, the juices will be bubbly.

**Note: We have a video demonstrating this. Search David the Good's videos on YouTube for how to peel a mango. For this recipe, I recommend not using David's peeling method.*

Mayonnaise

If you have chickens, you should have some eggs. If so, making mayonnaise is easier than you think. The mayo in the store is made from soybean oil and isn't good for you, so we don't buy it. Instead, we buy light olive oil and make our own mayo with eggs and lemon juice (or apple cider vinegar, if we don't have lemons or store-bought juice). Mayo is a very nice addition to many vegetable and root dishes and can be the base in other condiments, like homemade blue cheese dressing, salad dressings, and dipping sauces. Unfortunately, we've never grown enough olives to make our own olive oil, but – goals!

Homemade Mayonnaise

Yes. Just do it. Do you know what's in store bought mayo? Don't eat that stuff!!! This recipe is so easy and fool proof there's no reason not to make homemade mayonnaise. It does require a special tool, a submersible blender. But it's totally worth it!

Ingredients:

1 c. light tasting olive oil
1 egg
½ t. mustard of choice (my favorite is Grey Poupon)
1 T. plus 2 t. lemon juice (or apple cider vinegar of you are out of lemons or lemon juice)
½ t. salt

Find a 1-quart mason jar that is just slightly wider than your submersible blender. If it's not tight enough, it might not work. Place all ingredients into the mason jar. Put the submersible blender into the jar, all the way to the bottom, and start blending. The mayonnaise will instantly start to form on the bottom of the jar, mesmerizing everyone in the kitchen. Slowly lift the submersible blender to incorporate the unmixed oil at the top. Lift and plunge the mixer for a couple more seconds until it looks like mayonnaise. That's it! Use it on anything you would normally (or even not normally) put mayonnaise on!

**Note: Duck eggs make the most beautiful, yellow-tinted mayonnaise.*

**Another Note: This recipe has only failed to work for me on one occasion. I put a new egg in a new jar, poured the failed mayo on top, and blended again as described above. That fixed it.*

Moringa

Moringa is a fast-growing tree from Africa, grown for food, medicine and nutrition. We consume moringa regularly, both as fresh leaves and as dried leaf powder.

Moringa is definitely worth growing in Florida. In USDA growing Zone 8 and 9 your trees may freeze to the ground in winter. If the trees are well-established, however, they'll usually return, unless you get a wet winter. We had success growing them in the Gainesville/Ocala area. There are specimens in Gainesville that have regrown for 8+ years. Yet where we now live near Pensacola, winters are wetter and the stumps tend to rot in the ground. They have failed to survive two out of three winters.

Though you can start moringa from cuttings, David has discovered that seeds make much stronger plants. They're easy to germinate as long as the weather is warm – and they'll grow into a 10-20′ tree in a single growing season if conditions are good. Just don't overwater them when they are little, as the seedlings are prone to rotting.

You can start harvesting leaves from a tree that's only a few months old. To get some quantity, however, plant a group of multiple trees a few feet apart and keep cutting them back to make them bush out and produce more stems and leaves. A moringa hedge would be perfect for this!

In the Ocala area we once had a patch of 8 trees that made us about 4-5lbs of dried leaves every year. That's actually a lot of leaves, since they weigh almost nothing when dry.

That's enough to keep a family very well supplied with Moringa! We dried them in the house, and in the greenhouse as well.

If you water and fertilize well (just don't water too much when the trees first germinate – they'll rot), plus keep chopping shoots to encourage branching, you could probably get a pound or so of dried leaves from a year-old tree. We haven't had success harvesting the pods to use in dishes, as the trees have frozen in winter before fruiting in our North Florida gardens, but if you are in South Florida, you may be able to get some for the table.

Moringa leaves can be added to almost any dish. When raw, they are zippy, but when cooked they are mild in flavor and non-offensive. Soup, scrambled eggs, spaghetti sauce... just throw them in.

Or make tea!

Moringa Tea

Moringa makes a rich-flavored non-traditional tea.

You can dry the leaves and you'll get an earthy-flavored brew or simply boil fresh leaves. Strain the leaves out with a strainer and enjoy.

Making moringa tea from fresh leaves gives you a slightly zippy pot-liquor flavored brew that just tastes healthy. Add some honey for a sweet tea... or simply put it on ice like we do and enjoy the full flavor of nature's healthiest tree.

Mulberry

Mulberry is an often overlooked fruit tree that we absolutely love to grow. If you have a small space and are worried about a big purple mess, get a white-fruited variety! Mulberries fruit quickly when started from cuttings and provide lots of organic berries that children love to eat fresh.

If they don't all get eaten in the food forest, my older children often make them into a simple and delicious Southern cobbler that disappears in minutes.

Mulberry Cobbler

I cheated with this one. I took my Grandma's recipe for Cherry Mountain Pie and substituted mulberries.

Put all ingredients into a bowl and mix:

1 c. flour
½ t. salt
3/4 c. milk
1 c. sugar
1 ½ t. baking powder

Melt 1 stick of butter in the bottom of a 7 x 11" baking dish. Pour the above mixture over the butter.

Put one pound of mulberries into a bowl (no need to remove their green stems) and add a little sugar.

Stir to coat the mulberries with the sugar.

Scatter the mulberries on top of the cobbler batter.

Bake at 350 degrees for about 45 minutes or until golden brown.

Serve with vanilla ice cream.

**Note: If you are feeding a crowd, it is better to make 2 of these rather than to try to double it and put it in a larger pan.*

Nopale Cactus

Cactus aren't just a hot-weather desert plant. There are edible pad cactus spread across most of the United States, including Alaska. Most of us are familiar with the prickly pear fruit. Upscale grocery stores often carry them as a novelty in their fruit sections. The true prickly pear fruit is about the size of a plum with a rich red/purple juice and a berry-like flavor. Just watch out for the seeds – they're hard as rocks. A prickly pear is worth growing just for its fruit; however, it gets better than that.

The "pads" of the various *Opuntia* cactus are also edible. Most species we've tried are delicious. The flavor is somewhere between green beans and okra, with a little bit of saltiness to them. Some types are grown mostly for their pads since the fruit aren't great, like the "spineless prickly pear" *Opuntia cochenillifera.* David has grown this variety for years, though despite its "spineless" look, it does have awful little glochid spines on it that are almost invisible but sting and itch if you let the pads brush against you. If you pick the pads very young, before their spines develop, you're usually good to go – but if you pick them after spines appear, be careful. And the tiny glochid spines on many species are really, really annoying.

Some people will tell you that a blast of water is the best way to remove these little spines, but we don't trust it. Our favorite method is fire. Skewer a pad and turn it over an open flame. Voila! No glochids. Bigger spines are easy to remove with the end of a carrot peeler. Just core them right outta there.

Once the spines are gone, chop up the pads and use them however you like. We enjoy them in stir-fries and with eggs, like pretty much every other green thing that comes in from the garden, but David has made a chili with them that is really good.

Dave's Cactus Chili Of Death

Ingredients:

1-2 lbs ground beef or sausage
1 or 2 large onions
1 #10 can of kidney beans
A couple cans of tomato sauce or tomato paste and extra water
2-3 cactus pads with spines removed
Hot peppers
Spices and hot peppers and stuff

Fry ground beef/sausage in lard or tallow along with chopped up onions, some hot peppers and diced cactus pads in the bottom of a big pot. When cooked, pour in your beans and tomato sauce or paste. *You want it thin enough so it doesn't burn, but not so thin that the chili is watery.* At this point, add in as many of these things are you have available: Mexican seasoning, chili powder, paprika, ground red pepper, smoked hot pepper sauce (see recipe) or smoke seasoning, garlic powder, steak seasoning, Texas Pete hot sauce (or equivalent), black pepper and salt. Taste regularly to make sure you're balancing the flavors correctly. You want a meaty, smoky, spicy chili. Keep messing with it until it's perfect. *Serve in a big bowl with shredded cheddar and a dollop of sour cream.*

Serves roughly 8

As a final note on cactus, don't overlook them as an edible when prepping. They're widely available, have a hearty goodness to them, and they're easy to grow. To propagate, just find ones you like and plant their pads.

Below is a picture of Twice-stabbed Lady Beetles hunting pests on one of our Nopale cactus.

Okra

Neither David or I liked okra growing up. After we were married, we decided to try it again. People in Tennessee told us that the "only way to cook okra" was to slice it into rounds and bread and fry it so "it ain't so slimy." We tried that, and it was indeed good. But we didn't bother growing our own okra all that much. It wasn't until we moved to the island of Grenada that we started to really appreciate okra as a decent vegetable.

We first discovered a different good use for okra on our flight down to the island. We were flying Caribbean Airlines, and most of the staff seemed to be islanders. As part of the in-flight meal, we were served some sort of okra, tomato sauce and chicken dish that was really excellent. Once we settled in on the island, we realized lots of Grenadians were growing okra. It was a common vegetable, rather than being the fringe vegetable it is inside most of theUnited States. Only the South really seems to appreciate it here, with Louisiana being the stand-out state for okra lovers thanks to gumbo. Slimy? Who cares!

We started growing okra and experimenting with different methods of cooking it. David made pickles with it, which were entirely too slimy. I pan-fried it with breading and without breading. This was more palatable to the children. I also discovered that tomato-based okra dishes were often quite good, as we had first discovered on our flight.

When nothing else wants to grow in the heat and bugs of summer, okra marches on. Since it likes being here, we might as well learn to use it! And once you do learn to like it, you'll start looking forward to it every summer.

Stewed Okra in Tomato Sauce

If you think you don't like okra, try this. I bet you'll like it! The acid in the tomato sauce gets rid of the mucilaginous quality of the okra.

Ingredients:

A couple of handfuls of okra per person
enough tomato sauce or crushed tomatoes to give the okra a good sauce
garlic powder
onion powder
salt
pepper
Italian seasoning

Put a few tablespoons of fat in a pan over medium heat. Cut the okra into rounds about ¼ inch thick. Cook a couple of minutes. Add the crushed tomatoes or tomato sauce, garlic powder, onion powder, salt, pepper and Italian seasoning. I tend to be pretty heavy handed with the seasonings.

If the tomato sauce starts to pop out of the pan, reduce the heat. Cook about 10 minutes or until the okra is tender. Taste and adjust seasonings to your liking.

**Note: This is good served alongside chicken and rice.*

Simple Pan-Fried Okra

I don't like breading and frying anything. Don't get me wrong, I like eating it, as long as it's been fried in good fats. I just don't like frying it myself. It's just too messy and smoky. But I discovered that fried okra is just as good sans breading. And it doesn't seem to smoke up the kitchen.

Maybe it's the high temperature along with the fat that causes the okra not to be mucilaginous? I don't know. All I know is that it works, it's delicious and you won't have the spend an hour cleaning up the kitchen afterwards! Win!!

You want okra that is on the small-ish side. Bend the pointy end of the okra pod. If it snaps off like snapping the end off a green bean, it will be good to eat. If it bends and/or cracks, the pod is too mature and fibrous to eat.

Ingredients:

A handful or 2 of okra per person.
Several tablespoons of bacon fat/tallow/lard/ghee/coconut oil
Salt to taste

Cut the stem end off the okra and then cut the pods into rounds about ¾ of an inch thick. Fry in several tablespoons of hot fat until gently browned, string occasionally.

Transfer to a paper towel lined plate. Sprinkle with salt to taste.

**Note: You could also dust these with powdered Parmesan cheese.*

Papaya

We have eaten a lot of papaya over the years, both ripe and when green. It was basically a weed down in Grenada. The seeds would sprout in the rainy season and quickly grow into large trees, ripening fruit about a year after germination. We could pick all we liked, so long as we beat the parrots, rats and fruit bats to it!

We grew it in North Florida along the south-facing wall of our house with some success. Papaya really can't take the cold, so we often ended up with green fruits that we'd pick from the trees before frost. Even covering the entire tree wasn't always enough to keep the frost from blackening the leaves and destroying the fruit. Throughout South Florida, papayas grow quite easily but are often filled with grubs thanks to the obnoxious papaya fruit fly.

We quit growing them in the Great South Florida Food Forest Project since they needed too much protection to give us good, non-grubby fruit.

There's nothing sadder than opening up a nice, lovely, round, orange papaya and finding it completely filled with grubs.

If you protect the fruit from the fruit flies in the south, and the frost in the north, papayas can be very productive. Papayas are like a melon that grows on a tree (technically a plant) and are very enjoyable eaten fresh with breakfast in slices, or served with plain yogurt.

Ripe papaya is also very good when dehydrated.

If you have green papaya, they can be peeled and the inside pith removed, then sauteed like a vegetable. Or you can make green papaya salad like my Aunt Ja from Thailand. You'll find lots of recipes online. We don't have an original recipe that we use, since we only occasionally get papaya this far north.

A two-year-old papaya tree is easily capable of making 200lbs of fruit. You can plant a few seeds and get tones of fruit in a year under ideal conditions!

That's a lot of papaya salad!

Pear

There are pear varieties that grow well in Florida from about the middle of the state north. Many of them are called "sand pears," and are better used for processing than as fresh pears. Good varieties include Pineapple, *Moonglow* and *Orient*, though fresh eating types like Bartlett and Le Conte can be coaxed into growing provided the fireblight doesn't get them. Pears can be canned in syrup, dehydrated, used in place of apple in pies, and used as ammunition in large slingshots. Here are a few other great ways to use them.

Pear Sauce

Pear sauce is just like applesauce except with pears. I suppose it should be written "pearsauce," but there isn't a proper naming convention for such things.

To make pearsauce, just find an applesauce recipe and use pears instead. We don't like to add sugar, but make what tastes good to you, then you can jar it according to proper canning instructions and enjoy the taste of late summer all year round.

Pear Salsa

Two decades ago we left Florida for a time and bought a little house in Tennessee that had two pear trees in the yard. When they went into fruit, we had a flood of pears. Laundry baskets full!

We dried them, made pear sauce, made pear wine, canned pears in syrup... and yet, we still had more pears.

Looking for something different to do with them, we came across a recipe for "pear salsa" online. The batch we first made was too sweet and mild, but we made some changes and tried again, tweaking and remaking it over multiple batches to suit our palates.

Now, 15 years later, we have no idea what happened to the site we found that original recipe on, but it launched something great. What it's evolved into is really, really good and has become a favorite among our circle of friends.

Where we now live near the Gulf Coast, old sand pear trees are somewhat common. After Hurricane Sally, two different people gave us a bunch of pears and we got to make our pear salsa again, after missing it for years.

Now we've planted a half-dozen pear trees in our yard and we can't wait to have our own pears coming in regularly so we'll never be without the good stuff.

If you have extra pears, your family and friends will love this tangy-sweet, spicy-savory salsa. It's like nothing else you've ever had and is instantly addicting, despite the strange combination of ingredients. Though "sand pears," aren't the best right off the tree, when they're made into salsa they are heavenly. So, without further ado, here's...

The Best Pear Salsa Recipe Ever

Ingredients:

3 c. chopped onions
1 c. chopped garlic
4 c. chopped Red Bell Peppers
4 c. chopped jalapenos
5 quarts chopped hard pears
3 c. sugar
4 Tbsp salt
2 t. mustard seeds
1-2 t. smoked paprika
1 t. black pepper
1 t. ground cumin
2 t. cayenne pepper
A few c. of white or apple cider vinegar

Add everything to a big pot and bring to a boil. Simmer for 15 minutes, until the pears start to soften up. Season to taste – seasonings are approximate. If you like it spicier, chop and add a few habaneros or more cayenne pepper.

Transfer boiling salsa to canning jars and can. We can in a boiling water bath canner for 20 minutes.

Recipe makes roughly 10 pints of salsa. Serve with tortilla chips. Pear salsa is also great on pork chops.

Dehydrated Pears

Pears are very easy to dehydrate, and taste even better that way than when fresh.

Just peel and cut them into slices and put them in your dehydrator on the "fruit" setting. If you dry them too long they'll get crispy, but they're still good that way!

Store dehydrated pears in sealed jars, provided you can keep yourself from eating them all right off the dehydrator shelf.

Pecan

Though pecans are not thought to be a tropical tree, in *Create Your Own Florida Food Forest*, David shares the story of Bob Rose and two productive pecan trees in Hollywood, Florida. Their range is obviously larger than you might think, though pecans are more common in the panhandle where they are a staple of Southern living.

Chocolate Pecan Seminole Pumpkin Pie

I came up with this pie one Thanksgiving when I wanted to indulge in all my favorite holiday pies all at once.

For pie crust:

2 ½ c. white flour
½ t. salt
1 c. cold butter (2 sticks) cut into 32 pieces
1/3 c. cold water

Measure the water into a liquid measuring glass and place into the freezer while you work on the rest of the crust.

Put the flour and salt into a large bowl and whisk. Add the butter and crumble it together with your finger tips until it is all mixed in. Add in about half of the water and mix. You may need to use your hands. You want the dough to be soft and stick together. Add as much water as needed to achieve this. This recipe makes enough for a double crust, 9 inch pie. The Chocolate Pecan Seminole Pumpkin Pie calls for a 10 inch pie crust. So, when using it to make this pie, I make the crust as stated here and instead of separating it in half to use for the bottom of the pie pan, I would use a little more. Roll out the dough, place into the 10 inch pie pan and crimp the edge to create a high-standing rim.

For the chocolate pecan layer:

2 large eggs
½ c. cane syrup or maple syrup
4 oz semisweet chocolate
2 T. butter
½ t. vanilla extract
¼ t. Salt
1 c. coarsely chopped and toasted pecans

Preheat the oven to 400 degrees. Melt the butter and chocolate in a bowl in the microwave (or on the stove top in a double boiler). In a medium bowl, whisk eggs until foamy. Stir in chocolate mixture and other ingredients. Pour into the pie crust. Bake about 20 minutes or until the filling is set and slightly puffed.

Meanwhile...

For the Seminole pumpkin layer:

3 eggs
1 ¼ c. cooked pumpkin puree
1 c. milk
¾ c. packed brown sugar
1 ½ t. ground cinnamon
1 ½ t. ground ginger
½ t. salt
1 t. vanilla extract
pecan halves (optional garnish)

Put all ingredients for the Seminole pumpkin layer, except the pecan garnish, into the blender and blend until smooth. When the pecan layer of the pie is set, pour the Seminole pumpkin mixture on top of the still hot pecan layer. Return to the oven and bake about 40 minutes, or until the Seminole pumpkin is set in the middle. Garnish (optional) by pressing the pecan halves into the pumpkin around the edge of the pie. Serve with (unsweetened) whipped cream.

Sally's Plantation Pecan Pie

Sally was my Grandmother. I miss her so very much! This is her recipe. Or, at least I thought it was. But when I got the recipe card out to include it in this book I see she put a note at the bottom of the card. It states that it originally came from her sister Mary, my Great Aunt. Mary was an amazingly lovely woman; always smiling. So, as you make this pie, please pray for both their souls.

Ingredients:

1, 9 inch unbaked pie shell
2/3 c. white sugar
½ c. dark corn syrup
2 c. chopped pecans

3 eggs
½ c. white corn syrup
½ c. melted butter
24 whole pecans

Beat eggs; add sugar and mix well. Add syrups and butter and mix well. Add chopped pecans. Pour into unbaked pie shell. Arrange whole pecans on top. Bake at 350 degrees for about 1 hour or until and inserted knife comes out clean.

Ezekiel's Chocolate Chip Pecan Cookies

I started experimenting with cookie recipes a few years back to sell at my Dad's events. After making five or six different recipes with various success, I came across a recipe I liked. Over the past two years or so I have tweaked it for texture and taste. It upgrades your everyday chocolate chip cookie with pecans. The buttery texture will make your mouth melt. Perfect for picnics, parties, potlucks, and just about whenever your sweet tooth gets the best of you. -Ezekiel the Good

Ingredients:

1 c. butter, softened
1 c. white sugar
1 c. packed brown sugar
2 large eggs
2 t. vanilla extract
1 t. baking soda
2 t. hot water
½ t. salt
3 cups all purpose flour
2 cups semisweet chocolate chips
1 cup chopped pecans

Preheat the oven to 350 degrees F.

Mix butter, white sugar, and brown sugar together in a bowl. Beat in eggs, one at a time, and then add vanilla. Stir baking soda in hot water until dissolved, add this and salt to the batter. Mix in flour, chocolate chips, and pecans. Roll up the dough with your hands, or take spoonfuls of it, and set them onto a parchment lined, ungreased baking sheets, 2 inches apart. Bake for 10 minutes, or until edges are browned.

Cool them off for about ten minutes so you don't burn your fragile little mouth.

Enjoy!

Seminole Pumpkin

When a housewife thinks of pumpkins, she probably pictures Halloween decorations rather than food! Yet many pumpkins and winter squash are good to eat and taste a lot better than the flavorless pumpkins on sale in October. In Florida, the winning pumpkin is the native Seminole Pumpkin, a landrace *Curcurbita moschata* variety. Though its origins are murky, these pumpkins were reported as a native crop by the Spanish back in the 1500s, before the Seminole tribe from which it took its name. Seminole pumpkins come in varying sizes, shapes and patterns. Some weigh 12lbs or more and others only a few pounds. Some have necks and some do not. What connects them is their rampant growth and reliability, their resistance to diseases and vine borers, their rich orange flesh and long storage time. Seminole pumpkins can be added to soups, roasted in the oven, or baked into delicious pies. The taste of a Seminole pumpkin is much like that of a good orange sweet potato, rich and buttery. The seeds can also be roasted or fried in oil for a delicious snack.

We always have more Seminole pumpkins than we need, and they are a year-round staple in our house. (By the time of this year's harvest, we still had pumpkins sitting in the hall from last year – and this is common, as we grow a lot of them, and they keep incredibly well.)

Roasted Seminole Pumpkin

Cut a pumpkin in half, remove the seeds and bake in a 400 degree oven for about 45 minutes. It is finished when a butter knife goes in easily. We often serve these as a side, sliced into portions with butter and salt. Any leftovers I scrape out of their shells, mash with a potato masher and refrigerate. Use that in any recipe calling for "mashed pumpkin." It can also be frozen for future use. I have also had great success hiding it in curries, because it is already the same color as curry powder and blends right into the sauce. Shush! Don't tell the kids!

Seminole Pumpkin Banana Smoothies (See "Bananas & Plantains)

Jennifer Perry's Pumpkin Bread

This recipe comes from my fantastic mother-in-law, Jenni, who makes it every year around Christmas and gives it away to friends and family. Here I've adapted her recipe to compensate for the natural and varying sweetness of the Seminole pumpkin. You will be adding some sugar, tasting, and adding more to your taste. **Preheat the oven** to 350 degrees. Grease and flour three loaf pans.

Sift together:

3 1/3 c. flour
2 t. baking soda
1 t. nutmeg
1 ½ t. salt
1 t. cinnamon

Beat together:

1 c. softened butter
2/3 c. water
2 c. cooked, mashed pumpkin
1 t. vanilla
4 eggs

Add sugar, 1/4 to 1/2 c. at a time, to taste; mixing after each addition. Up to 3 c. Mix dry ingredients into wet ingredients. Pour batter into loaf pans and bake until done (approximate 1 – 1 ½ hours)

Pumpkin Waffles

Ingredients:

2 eggs, slightly beaten
¾ c. milk
¼ c. melted butter
½ c. pumpkin puree
1 ½ t. vanilla
1 c. all purpose flour
1 T. baking powder
1 ½ t. sugar
¼ t. salt
1 t. cinnamon
½ t. nutmeg
cane sugar, maple syrup, or powdered sugar for servings

Turn on the waffle iron so it's good and hot by the time your batter is ready.

In a large bowl, whisk together the flour, baking powder, sugar, salt, cinnamon and nutmeg. In another bowl stir together the eggs, milk, melted butter, pumpkin and vanilla.

Add the wet ingredients to the dry ingredients. Stir. Brush the pl[illegible] melted butter. Place enough batter onto the iron so that ¾ of the plate is [illegible] waffle iron. I find that my waffle iron takes ~6 minutes to cook. Experiment w[illegible]

As each waffle finishes, remove it from the iron and brush with melted butter.

Yield: 5 servings

*Note: *Topping the waffles with homemade cane syrup is fun as you can then use two crops from your homestead. However, I love the combined smell of the butter, powdered sugar and coffee. It smells like a diner.*

Seminole Pumpkin Soup

Ingredients:

5 c. of mashed pumpkin
4 c. of bone broth or chicken stock
1 dash nutmeg
1/2 cup cream (or coconut milk for an exotic twist)
Salt

Put mashed pumpkin into a pot with the bone broth stock. Bring to a simmer. Turn off the heat. Use an immersion blender for a really smooth texture (optional). Add cream and nutmeg. Salt to taste. **Serves 8.**

nerd's Needles

…ısy-like flowers that grow in your yard, which are then …spiky seeds that hook into socks and skirts? They're called …*ens alba.*

…ary food source for honeybees in the Sunshine State. But here's …t them: the leaves are edible! We pinch out the middle leaves and …efore they go into bloom. If they've already bloomed, we pick whatever leav… …k moderately decent. These leaves and shoots are good in stir-fries and we really like them cooked into scrambled eggs.

It's a free green from the yard and they're reportedly high in nutrients and medicinal value as well.

It may not be proper payback for all the little seeds that end up in the laundry pile, but at least it's something. Eat the weeds, as Green Deane says!

Starfruit

When we lived in the Caribbean, we went for a long stretch of time without a vehicle. We lived in a rented farm house about a mile up a rough mountain road, and some mornings David and one or two of the children would walk down to catch a bus into town and run errands and go shopping. The walk back up the mountain to our house was often undertaken in the middle of the day, when the tropical sun beat down. The road was rough and rocky and was steep enough to make you work up quite a thirst. Fortunately, in an abandoned lot just before you got to the house, there were three starfruit trees. Two of them had sour fruit, but one had sweeter fruit. When they were in fruit, which was about half the year, David would look for a starfruit to quench his thirst.

Starfruit are almost like eating crisp sweet-tart lemonade fruit. Sometimes the parrots would eat all of them off the trees by the house, but usually there were a few good ones for the picking. On the island, we didn't bother preserving them because there were so many fruit of various types to enjoy, but if you have a small yard and a lot of star fruit, they are worth keeping for the future if possible. They don't keep long on the counter, but can be cut into stars and dehydrated for a tasty snack.

They can also be made into...

Starfruit Jam

The following is a recipe from David's sister Christi. She shared her success with us and I asked her if she'd write up her recipe. The star fruit she used came from the beautiful and productive starfruit tree we planted in The Great South Florida Food Forest Project over a decade ago.

I looked at our beautiful starfruit tree and thought, "there are entirely too many starfruit to eat before they go bad."

I then thought "how could I let these sweet little fruits go to waste? David The Good would find a way to preserve them... that's it!"

So, preserve them I did! I picked a bucket full of star fruit and washed them with the care of a newborn babe. But before I get ahead of myself, here is the recipe and the play by play of how to make starfruit jam, or starfruit butter.

To me the texture was more like apple butter, but delicious nonetheless.

Ingredients:

8 ½ cups of fresh star fruit
3 c. of sugar

1 t. of vanilla
1 T. of lemon juice
2 t. of Cinnamon (I also added nutmeg and some allspice)
1 T. of butter

First, pick and wash starfruit. Cut off the ends of the fruit.

Cut the peaks of each ridge on the fruit.

Next, cut the remainder into roughly ½ inch cubes, removing the seeds as you go.

Boil the chunks in 4 cups of water or just add enough water until the starfruit is covered.

Now, add sugar, cinnamon, lemon juice, and vanilla.

Boil until the star fruit slices are soft.

Put this in the blender or blend with a submersible blender until smooth. Simmer to cook down into a thicker consistency.

Pour into jars and seal in water bath per Mason or Ball jar guidelines.

Let star fruit jam rest for 4 days before opening and eating.

This starfruit jam/butter is delightful. I made three small jars with this recipe. Next time you have too much starfruit to eat—consider making jam! (I don't know what is with me and working with foods that rhyme with yam.)

Until next time!

-Christine Faith Perry

Sugarcane

In Florida and much of the warmer South, "cane boils" are still part of rural country life. Sugarcane has a larger growing range than most people think! It's not just tropical, and can be grown as far north as Tennessee.

This means you can grow it anywhere in Florida. It doesn't have to be planted in a swamp. It will grow quite happily on high ground, so long as it gets enough water. We don't have to water ours most years since the rainfall is sufficient. One year we had a drought that lasted from the end of June into late Fall. That year we had a much lower yield, but the little canes were exceptionally sweet.

In North Florida, wait until it's just about time for the first frost of Fall or Winter, then go cut your canes down. This way, they have a long time to grow, and you'll get the largest harvest possible. If you don't cut them down and you get a freeze, you'll lose all the above ground growth and may even lose the plants. Harvest by cutting the canes down close to the ground, and then put the sugarcane roots to bed for the winter by mulching over them with some rough material.

In South Florida, just plant whenever you have planting material and keep them fed and watered. You can cut canes when they get nice and long, 6' or more. The leaves and top bit of a sugarcane stalk aren't sweet, so just chop that green part off and compost it.

The easiest way to enjoy sugarcane is to cut out the joints and peel the in-between sections and chew the sugary juice out of them.

Usually, though, backyard sugarcane is grown in the south to make cane syrup. And sometimes rum. Cane rum has a long history in the Caribbean and throughout Florida, but our current government sadly prefers taxable alcohol made by licensed distillers.

Fortunately, there's no restriction on making cane syrup, and it tastes better than rum on your pancakes.

The basics of making cane syrup are simple. Juice sugarcane and strain the juice. Then boil it under controlled conditions while stirring and skimming until it's boiled down to about 1/10th its original volume. Then jar it!

Here's a more in-depth look.

Homemade Cane Syrup

In 2022, we were invited to a cane boil at the home of Marcus Stewart in the Florida Panhandle. There, my family was able to help he and his own family and friends make a big batch of homemade cane syrup. David filmed a documentary on his method and interviewed Marcus on every step of the process.

Making cane syrup has a few hitches that are difficult to overcome on a home scale. When we made our own at home years before, we had to bypass the juicing process and simply cook the sugar out of the canes (more on that later). Juicing sugarcane is much better, however, and has a higher yield for much less processing time. If you can juice it!

Juicing sugarcane is actually quite difficult. It's hard to believe how tough the stems are under pressure, and it takes a literal ton (or more) of torque to pull off. We tried chopping up sugarcane into pieces and feeding it through our Champion juicer. No luck! It choked the machine, despite how incredibly tough that thing is. You really need a machine dedicated to juicing cane.

Marcus uses an antique Golden's Cane Mill he salvaged for a good price from an organization that had been using it as a yard decoration for years. He mounted it on a stand and attached a huge tree trunk to the top so it could be spun efficiently.

Marcus told us the crushing power of that machine is incredible. "Imagine a long-handled wrench and how much more force you get on a bolt," he said. "That's a massive amount of torque."

He uses a small Sears yard tractor to pull the post around the mill, but it can also be turned with a mule, an ox, or with someone who won't get bored walking around in a circle for hours.

This is his grinder rig:

Three canes at a time can be crushed by the mill, but no more. Their juice is directed down through cloth filters and into buckets, which, when filled are poured through a second cloth filter, then poured into the boiling kettle.

Juicing the cane is really the hardest part of this entire process. Once it's juiced, it's time for the boil.

Marcus boils his syrup in a 90-gallon cast iron pot. He laments not having a proper, wide "syruping kettle," but uses what he has. The actual boiling takes five or more hours. The goal is to evaporate away the water and thicken the sugarcane juice into delicious and shelf-stable syrup. A wider kettle allows for more evaporative surface.

As the syrup boils, scum is skimmed off the top.

After hours of boiling, the juice has thickened into rich amber syrup.

The syrup crew, in this case his son-in-law Joshua, checked the temperature regularly. As the water leaves, the boiling temp steadily rises higher and higher above 212, and when it hits a certain point, the syrup is judged to be finished. Our guess is that they pulled their syrup in the upper 220's. Other signs of the syrup being finished is the "clouding" of the boil and the bubble size, and when a "sheet" of syrup falls from an overturned dipper, instead of in individual drops.

At the proper thickness, the fire is rapidly pulled and the syrup is bottled in Mason jars for later sale.

It's an all-day event, and is more like a big family party than a work day. It certainly takes a lot of crushing and a lot of stirring, but there is a joy in the process when shared with friends and family.

There are some cheap "cane presses" for sale on Amazon, but we don't trust them. One day we hope to buy an old-fashioned crusher we can use in our yard to make our own syrup in large quantities.

If you don't have a cane press, you can still make syrup. Back in 2013, David explained our method on his blog. I worked it out via intuition, guessing that boiling chunks of cane would pull out the sugar, which could then be processed further – but earlier this year a visitor told us that her grandmother had done the same thing every year when she was a kid!

Here's David's explanation of the process.

How to Make Cane Syrup (without a Cane Press)

We've grown sugarcane here and there for roughly fifteen years.

The kids love it and it's a nice novelty but we always wanted to do more with our little crop than just hack chunks off for chewing.

Back in 2012 when I planted a big bed of sugarcane, I knew that at some point I'd have to figure out how to process it into something useful. Since distilling is apparently illegal, rum was out... but homemade cane syrup sounded like a winner.

Plus, Rachel wanted it, so it had to be made.

She was the one who guessed boiling the sugar out of the canes was the way to do it, too, and that's what we've done since. It's more time-consuming than using the juice, but you work with what you have!

Step 1: Harvest Some Canes

In North Florida there are freezes in winter that will knock sugarcane down to the ground, so we cut canes in November.

It's got to happen before frost or the crop will be ruined.

To harvest sugarcane, grab your machete and cut the canes close to the ground, then strip off the leaves and throw them over the short "stumps" left behind.

Because sugarcane is a cold-sensitive perennial, covering up the roots will keep the plant safe until next spring, when a whole new batch of homegrown sugar will rise from the ground when the soil warms up.

Step 2: Wash Those Canes

Sugarcane often has mildew on its stems, along with dust, dirt and the occasional bug. You don't want these in your syrup so we scrub the canes after removing the leaves. We do this over one of the garden beds and rinse with the hose as we go. We don't use soap; just water and elbow grease.

The canes are truly beautiful when they're wet – they look like lovely varnished bamboo.

Step 3: Start Chopping 'em Up

Here's the big problem with sugarcane: it's full of fibers. You can't just put chunks in your juicer. We tried... and I don't think our Champion juicer will ever be the same. After multiple jam-ups and some smoking and shaking which only yielded about a half-cup of syrup, we realized it was pointless.

Normally, sugarcane is processed with powerful presses that crush it flat and let the sugary juice run out. We don't have anything like this at home and couldn't figure out a good way to jury-rig something. Real presses are really expensive – and the Thai ones they often sell on e-bay are made for flattening squid, not crushing something as tough as sugarcane.

Don't waste your money! Just chop them into chunks instead.

A good heavy meat cleaver works well for this. We cut our canes into roughly 8" sections, then split those in half lengthwise.

Step 4: Boil the Chunks of Cane

After chopping, put the pieces into a large stockpot, cover them with water, then boil the sugar out of them. This takes some time and you have to make sure they stay covered with water, so top the pot off occasionally.

As the cane cooks, it will lose its lustrous color and start to turn pale brown. And the water will start to taste sweet. Once the flavor of the water is sweet and the cane tastes bland, you're ready to move on to the next step.

This takes an hour or two – let your tastebuds be your guide.

Step 5: Strain Out the Cane Fragments

Pour the hot sugary juice through a stainless steel strainer, which brings up a good point: **do this whole process with stainless steel implements, if you can at all help it.** Aluminum cookware leaches aluminum into your food, imparting off flavors while slowly poisoning you in the process.

You probably don't want aluminum fortified cane syrup.

Once you've poured off the juice into a second pot, it's time to *really* get cooking.

Step 6: Boil It Down

This step (and the previous one) makes your house smell amazing. It's not the molasses smell you would expect, though; it's more of a delicious sweet corn aroma.

You're going to boil... boil... boil this juice until the liquid has reduced in the pot to a dangerously low level. Just keep a half an eye on it and find something nearby to do, like the dishes.

If your juice hasn't thickened when the pot has boiled down to an inch or so in the bottom (mine is never thick enough at that point), then pour your big pot's contents into a smaller pot and proceed to the final step.

Step 7: Finish and Jar the Syrup

You're really close to the end now. It's the final stretch! At this point, you need to be careful not to let the syrup burn, turn into caramel or boil over. Cook it with constant supervision and be ready to pull it off the burner at a moment's notice.

The bubbles get very thick and glassy as it nears syrup consistency.

Our first batch trying this method was very, very thick so we learned to back off a little on the final boil down. We've also taken it too far and got a half-burned molasses-like syrup. It was still good on pancakes, but not as great as when you get it right.

At the end, repeatedly dip a spoon into the syrup and see how thick it is when it cools. Putting a few spoons aside in the freezer for this stage is a good idea. Once you've got the right thickness, pour your syrup off into a mason jar. Congratulations!

You've made your own home-grown, organic, vegan, free trade, sustainably harvested, locavore-approved, non-GMO, gluten-free, amazingly delicious sugarcane syrup!

Sure, it's a lot easier to juice the cane first, rather than doing the chop n' boil... but if you're just a hobbyist who wants a few jars of syrup to give away at Christmas, this beats having to buy a specialized extractor or find a local cane mill.

It would probably also work for sorghum... try it and see.

As a final note: homemade cane syrup tastes absolutely amazing... you're gonna try it and love it. I have no idea why it isn't as popular as maple syrup. In my mind they are neck and neck.

Happy syruping!

Sweet Potato

Sweet potatoes don't need sugar, and they most definitely don't need marshmallows!

If you grow your own orange sweet potatoes and give them a few weeks to "cure," the flavor goes from starchy to sweet. And when you then roast those sweet potatoes, the full delicious sweetness comes out. It's not marshmallow and brown sugar sweet, of course, but it's still good and sweet.

There are also tropical sweet potatoes with less sweetness, that tend more towards the starchy and the nutty in flavor. We currently grow white, orange and purple sweet potatoes, all of which have their own flavor. All are sweet, but the sweetest ones are the traditional orange variety.

Some people have written David and said that you could just use less-sweet sweet potatoes instead of white potatoes as a staple, but that hasn't been our experience. They're all somewhat sweet, so they don't fill in perfectly for white potatoes. Regular potatoes are better replaced by cassava and true yams – or even green plantains – but not by sweet potatoes! It just isn't right.

Well-cured sweet potatoes are sweet enough on their own without adding more sugar. Once you start to appreciate the way food really tastes without added sugar, you'll learn to love it.

David plants sweet potatoes in April, then lets them grow as big as possible before harvesting them in November or even December before our first freezes.

Though you'll see notes from agricultural extensions stating that sweet potatoes can be harvested in a few months, you can let them keep getting bigger for a lot longer through our long, Florida summer and warm Fall. Big potatoes are still great to eat.

That said, if you let them stay in the ground until the next year, they often get woody, bug-eaten and much less palateable.

Baked Sweet Potatoes

When David bakes sweet potatoes, he washes them, dries them, then rubs them with coconut oil or lard, then bakes them on the rack at about 400 degrees until they are fork-tender and the skins are getting crispy. I've found that I don't even need to oil the outside. I just wash them, then bake a dozen or more on a big pan at 400 degrees. At 45 minutes, I test to see how done they are. Big potatoes take longer than little ones, so you might have to take the little ones out first if you have mixed sizes.

Using Sweet Potato Leaves

Sweet potato leaves are edible when cooked. We saute them in stir-fries and add them to scrambled eggs. After pulling potatoes, we also feed the entire vines to our cows, pigs and chickens in Fall. People have seen us do this in our YouTube videos and always say "no, you can eat the leaves!" Yes, we know! But there's no way we'd ever eat all the leaves off those vines. Plus, our animals love them even more than we do. Think of the happy cows and chickens and hogs! They are good recyclers of all the extra we produce around the farm.

Wild Grapes & Muscadines

When you get a big basket of wild grapes, what do you do with them? When we picked wild muscadines along our fence line, most of the grapes were small, with a bunch of seeds in them. They are very sour, but also have a lot of grape flavor. Jam time!

Disclaimer: We've made jam, of one sort or another, every year, so for me the process has become a no-brainer. If you've never done it before, or you're a bit rusty, you might want to read up on some basics before jumping right in. Botulism isn't fun! Also, this is probably not the recommended, gourmet way to do this, but I don't really care. It works, and it's easy.

Wild Grape Jam

First, put all the grapes, stems and all, into a large pot along with about 1/4 cup of water. I turned it to high, and when it started to sound like the water was heating up, I turned it down to medium. I think a lot of recipes will tell you to start at medium or medium-low, but I'm impatient. I want things to get up and get going, but not burn. Just keep an eye out and you'll be fine.

Fill your largest, widest pot a little more than half-way full of water. Cover and bring to a boil. Turn the heat off but leave it on the burner.

Put all the spoons in your silverware drawer into your freezer. Yes you heard me right. Just go do it. You'll need them later.

While that's happening, get a bunch of half-pint jars out and wash them along with their lids and rings. Now here's a trick for you, the manufacturers of these lids will tell you that you can't use them over again.

IT ISN'T TRUE!

They can be reused over and over again, but you have to make sure they are sound! Test them. As long as the dome on the top will pop down *and up again*, they will work. Also, take a look at the rubber seal–the part that touches the top of the jar. If it makes contact with the jar all the way around its rim, it will work. The same goes for store-bought jars and lids. We've saved them from store-bought jam, salsa, you name it, so that we don't have to buy new jars each time we want to can something.

After the jars and lids are washed, sterilize them by putting them into the oven. I place the jars on top of a cookie sheet on the top rack of a cold oven and the lids into a pie plate below. Then turn the oven on to its lowest temperature. When the oven is finished preheating, the jars and lids are finished sterilizing. At this point I turn the oven off and leave them in there until I'm ready for them. I find this to be much simpler than dipping them all into boiling water.

With a potato masher, mash the grapes every now and again to help them release their juices.

When the grapes themselves have turned to mush, you're ready to strain your concoction. I used a fine mesh metal strainer and strained small batches at a time. If you have a food mill you could use that.

Once you've pressed out as much juice as your patience will allow, measure it.

The USDA publishes recommendations on all sorts of jams and jellies. I just looked up how much sugar to add per cup of grape juice and went with that. This is pretty important. If you don't get enough sugar in there, it can cause the jam to spoil–and you may not always be able to tell when that has happened.

Rinse out the large pot and put the juice back in along with the sugar and bring to a boil.

Reduce a tad to between a boil and a simmer, then sprinkle in a tablespoon of pectin. I prefer the little jars of "low to no sugar needed" stuff. Stir for about a minute. Now take one of the spoons from the freezer and drop a small amount of jam on it. Tilt it downward. If it sets up, touch it. Does it feel like the thickness of jam? Then you're finished with this step. If not, add another tablespoon of pectin, stir for another minute and re-test on a frozen spoon. Do this until you reach the desired consistency.

Turn the heat back on to high underneath the large pot of water.

Remove the jars from the oven and ladle in the hot jam. Wipe the rims clean of any sticky jam so the lids will have a good surface to stick to. Put the lids on, but don't over tighten them. Just finger tight will do. Use jar tongs to place the jars into the pot of boiling water.. The water should cover the lids. If it doesn't, add more. The USDA told me to boil these half-pints for five minutes. Different recipes and jar sizes call for different lengths of boil time. Be sure you look it up as this can effect how the jam keeps.

After the allotted time, remove the jars and listen. As they cool, the domes on their lids will pop down. After they have cooled, check to make sure they all popped. Any that haven't won't keep on the shelf but will last for a week or two in the fridge.

This rarely happens to me, but when it does, we just eat it right away. Label the jars with the month and year. They should keep in a room temperature, dark place for one year. When you take a new jar off the shelf, before you open it, make sure the dome is depressed. If it pops up and down, the seal has broken on the jar and you need to throw it away.

And there you have it: your own wild grape jam! This also works with homegrown muscadines, which are the only grapes that really grow well in Florida. Still, the wild ones are really fun to use when you can find them. Especially if you have good help!

Wild Plums

Multiple species of wild plum grow in Florida. The Flatwoods plum and the Chickasaw plum are the most common, though the wild American plum is also reported. We found these plum trees in a big stand by the highway on a road trip:

Keep your eyes open for white plum blooms by the road in Spring, then watch for fruit later!

Wild Plum Jam

To make wild plum jam, adjust the jam recipe used for wild grapes above. Tart wild plums make an absolutely delicious jam that is better than any sweet plum jam. The tartness and the sugar together are out of this world.

Yams

Most people in the US get yams mixed up with sweet potatoes, but they are most definitely not sweet – and they aren't even related to sweet potatoes! David says they are probably the easiest staple crop you can grow in Florida, and we always have them in our kitchen. We've been growing true yams for a little over a decade. Harvest season for yams is in the late fall and through the winter into early Spring, and that's when we have way more than we need.

Before we moved to Grenada, we made yam home fries and yam hash browns from fresh-cut yams, simply chopped or shredded and fried in hot oil. However, after doing the same thing with the same species of yam down on the island, we felt the scratchy tingle of oxalic acid crystals in our mouths when we ate them, so we stopped. Now David no longer recommends frying them directly since we know there are cultivars that have more oxalates in them.

It's safer to boil them, then dry and fry; like I explained doing with cassava.

Yam Fries

Wash yams, then peel with a peeler or knife. There are some oxalates in the yams that make my skin burn when I peel them without gloves, so I always use rubber gloves. The oxalates don't seem to bother David when he peels yams, so your mileage may vary. Once the yams are peeled, cut them into chunky pieces, then put them in a pot of water to boil. Once they are fork tender, strain them out and let them cool a bit. Now heat up some oil in a skillet and fry them until the outsides are crispy. Serve with your favorite dipping sauce (homemade mayonnaise is great!).

Mashed Yams

Wash yams, then peel with a peeler or knife. Cut them into good-sized chunks and boil until fork-tender. Now substitute them for potatoes in your favorite mashed potato recipe. Add extra butter, sour cream, and homegrown chives.

Chinese Yam Bulbil Fries

The Chinese yam is the only yam we grow that can be eaten without cooking. However, we don't usually use the roots. Instead, we gather the hundreds of tiny aerial bulbils that grow on the vines. They are about the size of a small marble and can be fried (peels and all) in oil (tallow is amazing!) and salted to make a very delicious snack or side dish. They're like tiny potatoes fried whole!

Yard-long Beans

Yard-long beans are the best green bean for Florida. They are productive, can take the heat, and they'll impress your friends. A single pod can grow as long as your arm! The green types we've grown taste better than the red or purple types, which were tougher and tasted like cardboard. They are great steamed, sauteed or eaten fresh in the garden. And they make a mean green-bean casserole.

Yard-long Bean Casserole

This is pretty much the classic green bean casserole you would find gracing Thanksgiving tables across the country, except that it uses yard-long beans. So if you have a favorite green bean casserole recipe, feel free to use it. If not, use this one.

Ingredients:

2 lbs of yard-long beans
3 T. butter
2 (10 ½ oz) cans cream of mushroom soup
¼ c. heavy whipping cream
1 ½ c. crispy fried onions, divided
2 oz. Parmesan cheese, grated (about ½ c.), divided

Preheat the oven to 350 degrees. And grease an 11x7 inch baking dish.

Cut the ends off the yard-long beans and cut them into 3 inch sections. Saute them in the butter, on medium-low, about 5 minutes.

Remove the yard-long beans and place into a large bowl. Add the soup, heavy cream, ½ c. of the onions and ¼ c. of the Parmesan cheese. Stir to combine.

Pour the yard-long bean mixture into the baking dish and top with the remaining 1 c. of onions and ¼ c. Parmesan cheese.

Cover with aluminum foil and bake 20 minutes. Remove the aluminum foil and bake another 20 minutes, or until the top is golden. Remove from the oven and let rest at least 10 minutes before serving.

Yield: 8 servings

As a final note on yard-long beans, just give them a good trellis right from the beginning. The vines are vigorous, though they take a little time to get running. Once they run, they'll go straight up about eight feet and pull over a wimpy trellis. Plan ahead! The cattle panel trellises we illustrate in *Minimalist Gardening* work really well for yard-long beans, and you can see the same design in one of David's YouTube videos.

Conclusion

Thanks so much, y'all, for asking me to write this book. It has been a blast putting it together and sharing our kitchen with yours. Over time, the "weird crops" that grow in Florida will become as familiar to you as carrots and potatoes. Stick to it, experiment, have fun – and be sure to come and visit us at thesurvivalgardener.com as we continue to grow.

About Rachel The Good

Rachel The Good enjoys cooking, eating and thinking up new ways to prepare the exotic produce her husband pulls in from the garden and food forest. Also in charge of managing a large household, she is always on the look-out for new ways to keep things simple. She lives somewhere a little north of Pensacola with her husband and 11 children.

Florida Gardening Books by David The Good

Create Your Own Florida Food Forest
Florida Survival Gardening
The South Florida Gardening Survival Guide
Totally Crazy Easy Florida Gardening

Additional Books by David The Good

The Easy Way to Start a Home-Based Plant Nursery
Grocery Row Gardening

Good Guides:

Compost Everything: The Good Guide to Extreme Composting
Grow or Die: The Good Guide to Survival Gardening
Push the Zone: The Good Guide to Growing Tropical Plants Beyond the Tropics
Free Plants for Everyone: The Good Guide to Plant Propagation
Minimalist Gardening: The Good Guide to Growing Food with Less

Gardening Thrillers:

Turned Earth: A Jack Broccoli Novel
Garden Heat: A Jack Broccoli Novel

Made in the USA
Columbia, SC
25 September 2024